Why You Need This New Edition

The Actor in You, Fifth Edition has been revised to bring you a simpler, more direct approach to learning the essential concepts of the art of acting. This newest edition provides the best user experience in discovering and enhancing your acting skills, including features such as these:

1. New material and many changes reflect user requests, especially a new ordering of the steps that gets you **up and at work sooner.**

2. Four part structure—qualities of a good actor, basic principles of acting for stage or screen, step-by-step approach to basic text analysis, and an outlining of the actual process of rehearsing and performing a scene—provides you with **a logical sequence** but also with **flexibility for instructors to vary the order** to fit their own approaches..

3. An expanded glossary at the end of the book allows you to be **up-to-date with** the most current concepts and terms in the field.

4. Complimentary teacher's guide, available at www.robertbenedetti.com, advises professors in how to save valuable class time for personal contact with you, to **minimize talk and maximize work time** in the classroom.

Fifth Edition

THE ACTOR IN YOU
SIXTEEN SIMPLE STEPS TO UNDERSTANDING THE ART OF ACTING

Robert Benedetti

The University of Nevada, Las Vegas

Allyn & Bacon

Boston   Columbus   Indianapolis   New York   San Francisco   Upper Saddle River   Amsterdam
Cape Town   Dubai   London   Madrid   Milan   Munich   Paris   Montreal   Toronto   Delhi
Mexico City   Sao Paulo   Sydney   Hong Kong   Seoul   Singapore   Taipei   Tokyo

Acquisitions Editor: Jeanne Zalesky
Editorial Assistant: Stephanie Chaisson
Managing Editor: Linda Mihatov Behrens
Associate Managing Editor: Bayani Mendoza de Leon
Manufacturing Buyer: Clara Bartunek
Marketing Manager: Wendy Gordon
Creative Art Director: Jayne Conte
Project Coordination, Text Design, and Electronic Page Makeup: Sudip Sinha, Aptara®, Inc.
Cover Designer: Bruce Kenselaar

Cover Image: On the cover: Savannah Smith as The Moll in the author's 2009 production of
Marc Blitzstein's *The Cradle Will Rock* at the Nevada Conservatory Theatre, University of
Nevada, Las Vegas.

Library of Congress Cataloging-in-Publication Data

Benedetti, Robert L.
    The actor in you : sixteen simple steps to understanding the art of acting / Robert
Benedetti.—5th ed.
        p. cm.
    Includes bibliographical references and index.
    ISBN-13: 978-0-205-78123-2
    ISBN-10: 0-205-78123-3
    1. Acting.   I. Title.
    PN2061.B392 2012
    792.02'8—dc22

                                                                                        2010020498

1 2 3 4 5 6 7 8 9 10—CRS—13 12 11 10

Allyn & Bacon
is an imprint of

www.pearsonhighered.com   ISBN-13: 978-0-205-78123-2
                                 ISBN-10:   0-205-78123-3

CONTENTS

NOTES ON THIS FIFTH EDITION

My first acting book, *The Actor at Work*, was written forty-five years ago and is now in its tenth edition. It presents a wide-ranging and detailed training program for the aspiring professional actor. Though widely used, teachers reported that *The Actor at Work* was too detailed and too advanced for many beginning students and for students who wanted to enhance their appreciation of acting without necessarily embarking on a professional career. I decided, therefore, to write *The Actor in You* specifically for these students.

Teaching beginning acting requires a crystal clear understanding of the acting process; to write *The Actor in You*, I had to identify the most crucial elements of the art, find a way to express them in simple language, and arrange them in a logical and effective sequence. This process was a valuable experience for me, and with the assistance of reviews written by classroom teachers and professional actors who have used the book, the four subsequent editions have extended my own developing understanding of the art of acting in all its forms.

NEW TO THIS EDITION

This new fifth edition of *The Actor in You,* has been revised to bring students a more simplistic and direct approach to learning the essential concepts of the art of acting. This new edition provides the best user experience for students who are discovering and enhancing their acting skills, and further allows them to see the ways in which they can hone the acting skills they already possess. New material has been added and suggestions from reviewers have been incorporated into this edition, particularly through a re-ordering of the steps. The four part structure, which includes qualities of a good actor, basic principles of acting for stage or screen, a step-by-step approach to basic text analysis, and an outlining of the actual process of rehearsing and performing for the scene provides students with a logical sequence in which to learn, while leaving room for instructors to vary the order to fit their own teaching approaches. An expanded glossary is included at the end of the book helps students stay up-to-date with the most current concepts and terms in the field. Finally, an updated complimentary teacher's guide is avaiable at www.robertbenedetti.com, which guides professors on how to make the most of valuable classtime.

PREFACE

This fifth edition has been revised according to suggestions from users of the previous editions. It offers sixteen easy steps that lead to an understanding and experience of the acting process. It is designed for students at the introductory level, whether they are beginning a training process as actors or merely want to enhance their understanding and appreciation of the actor's art.

The sixteen steps are arranged in four parts that form a logical sequence, though instructors may wish to vary the order to fit their own approaches. Part 1 begins with a description of the qualities of a good actor and a brief history of the acting tradition. We then get right to work with warm-ups and basic body and voice work, as well as enjoyable exercises to prepare for creative group work in a relaxed and effective way. Part 2 then uses examples drawn from everyday life to explain the basic principles of acting for stage or screen; each concept is put to work in a simple improvisational or game-playing exercise. Part 3 offers a step-by-step approach to basic text analysis as students begin to prepare a simple, short, contemporary scene. Part 4 outlines the actual process of rehearsing and performing the scene.

Throughout, examples are used from four widely available plays: Arthur Miller's *Death of a Salesman*, Lorraine Hansberry's *A Raisin in the Sun*, Luis Valdez's *Zoot Suit*, and Tennessee Williams's *The Glass Menagerie*. I urge you to read each of these plays in order to better understand my examples. In addition, a scene from the television show *Cheers* is provided in Appendix A. I also refer to *The Poetics* of Aristotle several times which, I recommend as the single most influential work in the history of Western drama.

GLOSSARY

Many stage and film/TV terms are defined in the glossary at the end of the book. These terms are in **boldface** when they first appear in the body of the text.

TEACHER'S GUIDE

A free teacher's guide can be downloaded at www.robertbenedetti.com.

ACKNOWLEDGMENTS

My thanks to the many students and colleagues who have contributed to my understanding of the acting process, either by their teaching or by their artistry. Thanks also to those who reviewed the manuscript for this edition: professional actor Henry Clarke, Stacy Alley, Arkansas State University; Sara Nalley, Columbia College; Murray McGibbon, Indiana University; Stephen A. Schrum, University of Pittsburgh at Greensburg; Franklin J. Lasik, University of Missouri; Cheryl Kennedy McFarren, Denison Univeristy.

ABOUT THE AUTHOR

A distinguished teacher of acting and directing, and recipient of multiple Emmy and Peabody Awards for film production, Robert Benedetti received his Ph.D. from Northwestern University. He was an early member of Chicago's Second City Theatre and then taught acting for over forty years at schools including the University of Wisconsin–Milwaukee, Carnegie Mellon University, the National Theatre School of Canada, and the University of California–Riverside. He was Chairman of Theatre at York University in Toronto, head of the acting program at the Yale Drama School, and Dean of Theatre at the California Institute of the Arts. He is currently a tenured full professor at the University of Nevada–Las Vegas and artistic director of the Nevada Conservatory Theatre.

Dr. Benedetti has directed at many regional theaters—including the Tyrone Guthrie Theatre; the Oregon, Colorado, and Great Lakes Shakespeare festivals; and the Milwaukee, San Diego, and South Coast Repertory Theatres—and overseas at the Melbourne, Australia, Repertory Theatre and the Berlin Festival.

As a film writer and producer, he won three Emmys and a Peabody award for producing *Miss Evers' Boys* and *A Lesson before Dying* for HBO, and he has written and produced numerous other films.

Dr. Benedetti has written six books on acting and film production, including *The Actor at Work, ACTION! Acting for Film and Television*, and *From Concept to Screen*. In 2005 he received the Lifetime Career Achievement Award from the Association for Theatre in Higher Education. His first novel, *The Long Italian Goodbye,* was published in 2005; his second, *Dynamite and Roses,* in 2009. He can be reached at www.robertbenedetti.com.

PART ONE

Preparing Yourself to Act

There are many reasons to study acting. You may be considering a professional acting career; you may think the study of acting will help you present yourself more effectively in everyday life; or you may simply wish to better understand acting in order to enhance your enjoyment of plays, films, and TV shows. Whatever your reason, you will discover that the study of acting can also be a process of self-exploration that can expand your spiritual, psychological, and physical potential. Brian Bates, a psychologist who also teaches acting, lists some of the ways in which the study of acting can contribute to personal growth:

> Finding our inner identity. Changing ourselves. Realizing and integrating our life experience. Seeing life freshly and with insight into others. Becoming aware of the powers of our mind. Risking and commitment. Learning how to concentrate our lives into the present, and the secrets of presence and charisma. Extending our sense of who we are, and achieving liberation from restricted concepts of what a person is.[1]

This last, *achieving liberation,* may be especially important to you if you feel limited in your behavior and emotional life by influences from your upbringing, peer group, or cultural tradition.

Even if the study of acting serves no immediate personal purpose, it can give you an enhanced understanding of real-life behavior, especially the way people act and react in pursuit of their needs and desires. Drama is the one art that is entirely concerned with the way

---

[1]Brian Bates, *The Way of the Actor* (Boston: Shambhala, 1987). p. 7.

people think, feel, and interact with one another and with their world. Great plays from all times, places, and cultures reveal to us the underlying patterns and truths of the human condition, including our own.

In all these ways, the study of acting, even if it does not lead to a professional career, is a meaningful journey of personal discovery and self-expansion. Through acting you can explore your own thoughts and feelings, have experiences far beyond what your real life offers you, live in new worlds, and say and do things you would never be able to experience otherwise. What a wonderful adventure!

1

Understanding the Actor's Job

In the simplest sense, an actor is anyone who performs a role in a play, TV show, or movie. Each of these three media—stage, small screen, and big screen—requires its own techniques, skills, and approaches, and few actors are equally good at all of them. A good TV sitcom actor, for instance, may not do well in a dramatic feature film, while an accomplished feature film actor may fail to deliver a stageworthy performance in a live theater. Moreover, the many different kinds of material performed in each medium make different emotional and technical demands on actors, and again, not every actor is good at all of them. An accomplished comic actor, for instance, may not do well in a serious role, and vice versa. Regardless of the medium and type of material, however, there are certain basic things that *all* good actors in all media and with all types of material must be able to do. These fundamental skills will be the aim of our study in this book, as step by step we lay a foundation on which future work may be based.

The first thing we might think all actors must do is to be *entertaining*. Certainly an actor must sometimes be entertaining in the popular sense, but this term fails to distinguish actors from the whole range of other kinds of performers who provide entertainment. We expect from a good actor a wide range of experiences, depending upon the nature of the material being performed.

Another common understanding of the actor's job is to create *emotion*. Certainly the actor's work will often involve and produce emotion, but as you will see in Part 2, emotion is only one by-product of the actor's creative process and is never an end in itself. Focusing on emotion for its own sake, as you will come to understand in later steps, is an unreliable and false way of working.

Yet another common perception of the actor's job is that he or she creates a *character*. Certainly this is a major aim of all actors, but again it is the result of the acting process, not a starting point, and not even the whole aim of the actor. The good actor not only strives to show us who the character is, but also invites us to experience the character directly through our participation in the character's behavior and the thoughts behind that behavior.

Moreover, the actor does this to fulfill the purpose for which the character was created in the telling of the play's story. A character never lives unto him- or herself, separate from the story of which the character is a functioning part, and the good actor is never concerned with the creation of a character that stands apart from the world of the play and the function of that character within that world. In this sense, the actor is also involved in *storytelling*.

In addition to all of this, every good actor strives to create a performance that is *engaging,* that draws the spectators in and compels their attention in whatever way is required by the material. This engagement is what makes all the other components of the actor's work—emotion, character, and story-telling—possible. Let's begin, then, by considering what makes a performance engaging.

ENGAGEMENT

In 350 BCE Aristotle became the first Western philosopher to describe the qual-ities of a good play, and one of the qualities he believed was necessary was *sympatheia,* or "fellow-feeling," the ability of the audience to recognize the characters as fellow human beings. This is what we commonly call "believabil-ity." Notice, however, that believability is relative to the style, content, and in-tent of the material being performed. Naturalistic plays, fantasies, slapstick comedies, classical tragedies, sitcoms, political satires, and the wide range of other performance forms all create their own worlds, each with its own sense of believability, some far removed from the appearances of everyday life. In all media and types of material, it is the world of the story that establishes what is "real," and the actor's performance must be believable within that world.

Whatever the demands of the specific material, however, an engaging per-formance always connects with us in a personal way; it draws us in and makes us feel as if we are "in" the characters and their world. This sense of engage-ment on a personal level is called **empathy**, which means "in-feeling." Empathy is not the same as sympathy; we can feel "in" a character even if the character is unsympathetic (indeed, some of the most vivid characters in the history of drama are villains). Given a good performance by the actor, we can empathize with a character even if his or her values, behavior, and world are very different, even antithetical, to our own.

This, in fact, is one of the great values of the dramatic experience: we can learn much about ourselves by feeling what it is like to do things, hold values, and live in worlds that are foreign to us. American director Zelda Fichandler likened doing a play to an archeological dig, since the acting and directing processes enable both makers and spectators to venture into different times, places, values, and behaviors and experience them first-hand. This is especially true of older plays and plays from other cultures, but even a contemporary play can offer new insights into our own world and behavior, helping us to see the familiar in new ways.

In fact, most actors especially enjoy playing roles that require them to reach out into new experiences and to explore new, dormant, or hidden aspects of themselves; one of the greatest rewards of being an actor is this unending opportunity for self-discovery and self-expansion. The actor is, in a way, an explorer of the human psyche and condition; he or she journeys into the life of the character and the character's world and then reports back to us by embodying the essence of what has been discovered, expressed in a heightened and purified form.

When the actor accomplishes this, the spectator is invited to go along on the journey of exploration and become personally engaged, experiencing the character and the character's world and the events that occur there "as if they are before our eyes," as Aristotle put it. This **immediacy**, he felt, was the essential quality of great drama and distinguished it from all other forms of literature and performance. A great play well performed is not *about* an event; it *is* the living event itself "as if before our eyes." For this reason we will, in the first steps, emphasize the need for the actor to work in the here and now. The immediacy of the dramatic performance is potentially memorable and life-changing; at its best, theater creates something truthful that will live on in the audience's very being.

TRUTHFULNESS

Aristotle wondered why we eagerly watch a play that presents a painful spectacle, such as the tragedy *Oedipus Rex.* How can such an awful experience attract us? Aristotle's answer was that we can enjoy a painful play because we learn something truthful from it, and learning the truth, Aristotle believed, is "our greatest joy." Therefore, we can say that the best kind of actor *engages the audience in order to communicate truth.* Even material meant to be a pleasant escape, such as a TV sitcom, is more valuable and enjoyable if it offers some measure of truthfulness and insight. Indeed, the greatest sitcoms—such as *M.A.S.H., Cheers, Seinfeld*, and others—all contained truth. One in particular, *All in the Family,* with its character Archie Bunker, made real changes in American society.

It is difficult to express precisely what we mean by the idea of "truth" in art, perhaps hardest of all in theater, film, and television, which function as both commerce and art. The commercial demands of the media are often at odds with the desire to present truth, and much commercially successful entertainment contains no truth at all—some even reinforces false and destructive stereotypes. It is left to the ethical commitment and skill of each artist to ensure that truth somehow survives commercial pressures. We often speak of the actor's physical and vocal skills as his or her **craft**, and it is interesting that the word *craft* comes from the German word for "power." Through his or her skill, the actor has the potential power to affect the lives of the spectators, and it is the ethical responsibility of the good actor to use this power for a meaningful and truthful purpose. Like the doctor, the actor should "first do no harm."

It is easier, perhaps, to say what theatrical truth is *not*: It is not an obsequious appeal for the audience's favor at any cost; it is not the reinforcement of stereotypes that deny the uniqueness of individual human beings; it is not propaganda that distorts reality in favor of a particular point of view; it is not mere impersonation that mimics the appearances of everyday life, however believable they may be, without expressing some deeper insight; it is not the creation of an emotional state for its own sake, no matter how moving it may be; it is not a selfish display that distracts from one's fellow actors or the meaning of the story.

Truth is a personal matter driven by the life experience of each artist, and part of a serious professional actor's job is to discover what he or she recognizes as truthful in a performance and what he or she has to say about the human condition through acting. The work of all the great theater makers throughout history has been based on their search for truth, and their techniques were attempts to find the best ways to express that truth: The naturalism of Stanislavski, the presentationalism of Meyerhold, the demonstrative epic style of Brecht, the heightened physicality of Grotowski, and the many other ways of making theater were all an effort to find and express theatrical truth.

Whatever truth these varied approaches to acting tried to communicate, they all had in common the wish to create and present experiences that would relate directly to the lives of the spectators in a meaningful way and perhaps even have the capacity to change them, and thus change society. Stanislavski put it this way:

> You must love your chosen profession because it gives you the opportunity to communicate ideas that are important and necessary to your audience . . . to educate your audience and to make them better, finer, wiser, and more useful members of society.[2]

There is yet one more way that great acting serves us. While a good performance can give us insight into human behavior and enable us to recognize and better understand our own behavior and that of others, watching an actor create a new personal reality, a new self, can also remind us that we, too, have that same capacity. Whatever a play or film may teach us about who we *are*, the actor's capacity to transform him- or herself into a new character reminds us who we may *become*, that change and personal growth is possible.

A good actor, then, strives to create a performance that is both engaging and truthful—that is, relevant and useful to the lives of the spectators and thereby to the world—within the demands of the particular performance.

---

[2]Nikolai Gorchakov, *Stanislavski Directs* (New York: Funk & Wagnalls, 1954), p. 40.

SKILL

When Aristotle wondered how we can enjoy watching a tragedy, he said that besides the truth the experience offers, we can also enjoy the *skill* of the performer. Notice, however, that although great acting requires great skill, the actor's skill should never draw attention to itself in the sense of showing off or trying to get the audience's attention in inappropriate ways. The qualities that attract us to great actors are the same things that make us watch great athletes: their seemingly effortless skill, their total concentration on the job at hand, and their tremendous sense of aliveness. We marvel at the "artlessness," the transparency of the actor who can transport us completely into the world of the story. Actors who are able to work in this way become compelling; we sometimes say that we can't take our eyes off them.

In a basic way actors do things we all do: They speak, move, and have thoughts and emotions. What makes actors special is not so much *what* they do, but the special *way* in which they do it. You already have many of the basic skills you need to be an actor; what you need to begin to learn are the actor's special ways of using those skills in a *heightened* and *purified* way. A sociologist noticed this fifty years ago when he said:

> It does take deep skill, long training, and psychological capacity to become a good stage actor. But . . . almost anyone can quickly learn a script well enough to give a charitable audience some sense of realness. . . . Scripts even in the hands of unpracticed players can come to life because life itself is a dramatically enacted thing. . . . In short, we all act better than we know how.[3]

Nonetheless, performing for the stage or camera requires that these everyday abilities be heightened, purified, and brought within the control of a purposeful discipline. As the psychologist quoted earlier put it:

> Almost everything that actors do can be identified with things we do in less dramatic form in everyday life. But in order to express the concentrated truths which are the life-stuff of drama, and to project convincing performances before large audiences, and the piercing eye of the film and television camera, the actor must develop depths of self-knowledge and powers of expression far beyond those with which most of us are familiar.[4]

This book will help you begin to develop your everyday acting skills into the greater power of artistic technique. Your job is to recognize, focus, and strengthen the natural actor you already are. Only you can do this, but the ideas

---

[3]Erving Goffman, *The Presentation of Self in Everyday Life* (New York: Doubleday, 1959), pp. 71–74. Copyright © by Erving Goffman.
[4]Brian Bates, *The Way of the Actor* (Boston: Shambhala, 1987), p. 7.

and exercises in this book provide insights and experiences to help you fulfill your natural talents.

DRAMATIC FUNCTION

It is not enough for an actor to be engaging, truthful, and skillful. A good performance must also contribute to the particular story being told. Every character in a story has been created by the writer to do a certain job within the world of that story. There are many things characters may be created to do: They may move the plot forward, provide an obstacle to some other character, provide information, represent some value or idea, provide comic relief, and so on. Whatever the character was created to do, the actor must above all else create a performance that successfully does that particular job. We will call this the **dramatic function** of the role. Fulfilling this dramatic function is the most important responsibility of a good actor.

To sum up what we have said so far, all good actors strive to fulfill the dramatic function of their role in an engaging, truthful, and skillful way that is relevant and useful to the lives of the spectators and is within the demands of the particular performance. That's a tall order to be sure, and not even the best actors achieve all of it in every performance. But these are the qualities that all good actors strive for in their work.

> ### EXERCISE 1.1: WRITING A FILM OR TV REVIEW
>
> Pick a performance you have seen recently in a film or TV show that made a strong impression on you. Write a review of the performance that examines the qualities discussed thus far. In what ways was the actor *engaging?* Did you feel yourself to be *in the character's place* and in his or her world? Was the performance *skillful* without calling attention to itself? Was it *truthful* within the world and manner of the story? Did it serve the *dramatic function* of the character within the story? What did you learn about your own life from this performance?

DISCIPLINE

Finally, we must consider the quality that is most necessary to an actor's long-term growth and development in mastering the art of acting—*discipline*. Real discipline is not a matter of following someone else's rules. In the best sense, it is your acceptance of responsibility for your own development through systematic effort. You accept this responsibility not to please someone else, not to earn a grade or a good review or a job, but because you choose to become all that you can be.

Discipline is rooted in your *respect* for yourself, as well as your respect for your fellow workers, for your work, and for the world you serve through that work. Poor discipline is really a way of saying, "I'm not worth it" or "What I do doesn't matter." Discipline will come naturally if you can acknowledge your own value, the importance and seriousness of your work, and the great need for your work in the world.

Discipline also involves *regularity*. Your work, especially on technical skills, must be a daily affair. Stanislavski, looking back late in his life, had this to say:

> Let someone explain to me why the violinist who plays in an orchestra on the tenth violin must daily perform hour-long exercises or lose his power to play? Why does the dancer work daily over every muscle in his body? . . . And why may the dramatic artist do nothing, spend his day in coffee houses and hope for the gift [of inspiration] in the evening?[5]

Patience and a sense of striving together, being willing to accept the momentary failure for the sake of the long-term success—these are the attitudes you must nurture. The pressures of our educational system and of performance itself work against these attitudes, as does the normal desire of all of us to succeed. Resist these pressures. Enjoy your freedom as a student to explore a variety of approaches and experiences. Enjoy the journey, the exploration itself.

Summary of Step 1

All good actors, whether on stage or screen, strive to create characters that fulfill the dramatic function for which they were created, and they strive to do so in an engaging, skillful, and truthful way in order to provide insight into the human condition that is relevant and useful to the spectator. This requires discipline, which is rooted in respect for self. It also requires acceptance of responsibility for personal development through systematic effort.

---

[5]Constantin Stanislavski, *My Life in Art*, trans. J. J. Robbins (New York: Theatre Arts Books, 1952). Copyright © 1924 by Little, Brown & Co. and 1952 by Elizabeth Reynolds Hapgood.

2

The Tradition
of the Actor

As you begin your study of acting, you should be aware of the long tradition to which the actor belongs. A sense of tradition can inform and enhance your work and can be a great source of energy and courage.

Our Western acting tradition began in ancient Greece when towns would send male choric groups to compete against one another in the recitation of poems at religious festivals held in honor of Dionysus, the god of wine, transformation, and the life force itself. Gradually, the chorus leader began to speak as an individual character, and many historians consider this chorus leader to be the prototype of the actor. Eventually, two other actors were added, thus creating dialogue, and so plays as we know them were born. In 534 BCE a contest for tragedy was established in Athens and was won by the first known actor, Thespis; the word *thespian* comes from his name. Performing in large outdoor amphitheaters, these early actors wore masks to indicate the characters they played, and each actor appeared in several parts.

Over the next thousand years, the center of our Western theater tradition shifted from Greece to Rome. The Roman actors no longer wore masks, and plays became more spectacular, as well as more violent and licentious. When the Roman Catholic Church rose to power, it outlawed the theater, and around 400 CE actors were excommunicated. They remained outside the graces of the church—and polite society—for more than a thousand years thereafter.

Actors survived the Middle Ages mainly as traveling troubadours, telling stories in verse and song. These itinerant performers served the important function of carrying local dialects from one region to another, helping to create the national languages of Europe and England as we know them today.

The rebirth of the theater began in the 900s with brief playlets telling biblical stories performed in Latin by priests and choirboys as part of church services. Beginning in the 1200s, religious plays were expanded and moved outdoors; the actors were no longer priests or choirboys but members of nonreligious organizations such as trade guilds, like the rustics portrayed in Shakespeare's *A Midsummer Night's Dream*. Meanwhile, in the universities, plays were being written imitating classical Greek drama; these were produced in small private theaters for the aristocracy and were often performed by the courtiers themselves.

The rebirth of the professional actor happened about this time, not in the church or university, but in the banquet hall and courtyard. The nobility began to accompany dinners and other social events with comedic skits and legendary stories acted out by skilled performers. To provide these performances, troupes of actors began to travel from household to household, like the players in Shakespeare's *Hamlet,* performing comical interludes based on folktales. Meanwhile, in Italy the Commedia dell'Arte featured a traditional cast of characters and improvised dialogue. All these kinds of traveling players performed for nobility but also sometimes in market squares and at public festivals, eking out a living from their craft.

In England Elizabethan plays developed in the late 1500s when a new group of playwrights merged the interludes performed by wandering actors with the classically inspired plays of the universities. To perform these plays, companies of professional actors were formed under the sponsorship of nobles, and the business of public theater as we know it was born. The actors in these companies received regular salaries, and the leading actors were shareholders who received a portion of the box office income, much like today's movie stars who have profit-sharing deals.

Acting continued to develop as a profession throughout the 1600s with the emergence of companies run by strong actor/managers. Up to this time, all female parts had been played by young boys (there were even all-boy companies), but in the 1660s actresses began to appear regularly on the English stage. For many years these actresses were widely regarded as women of loose morals. In fact, up to that time both male and female actors were still denied burial in consecrated ground.

During the 1700s actors became increasingly important and respectable. Audiences were attracted to star performers rather than to particular plays. In the 1740s David Garrick brought greater realism to English acting, although the dominant style of acting for the next 150 years would seem artificial by today's standards.

THE TWENTIETH CENTURY

It was not until the turn of the twentieth century, with the work of Constantin Stanislavski (1863–1938) and his Moscow Art Theatre, that the truly modern actor was born, an actor devoted to searching for the truth of human behavior through systematic discipline and to making the world a better place through the ideas and experiences an actor could bring to an audience. Stanislavski's approach soon established itself as the dominant technique from his time to the present day. In its earliest form, Stanislavski's work stressed psychological and emotional techniques that encouraged the actor to work "from the inside out." Later, however, he switched to a more physical approach called the Method of Physical Actions. Throughout his life, Stanislavski continued to change and develop his "system."

Over many years, Stanislavski's Method began to spread as his books were translated from the Russian and actors who had worked with him traveled to other countries. In the United States, a number of acting teachers developed their own versions of Stanislavski's work, each emphasizing various features drawn from different stages of its development. Through the work of teachers like Lee Strasberg, Sanford Meisner, Uta Hagen, and others, various forms of the Method, some quite different from one other, became influential in the American theater of the mid-twentieth century. Few of these reflected the entire breadth of Stanislavski's own lifelong search and development, and it is only recently that we are coming to appreciate the whole arc of his work.

A contemporary of Stanislavski's, Vsevolod Meyerhold, (1874–1940), reacted against Stanislavski's approach and developed another kind of acting that borrowed from Asian theater and the storytelling spirit of the itinerant performer. Where Stanislavski's aim was to represent the truth of behavior through representational means, Meyerhold's theater was presentational and overtly theatrical. Focused not on the psychology of behavior but on the structure of the body, Meyerhold's central discipline was called *biomechanics*. It used physical training to forge the connection between mind and body, to "teach the body to think." It began with simple activities like running and jumping and then progressed to leaps and rolls, movement with objects, movement up and down ramps and stairs, partner lifts, and acrobatics, culminating in highly stylized movement pieces choreographed by Meyerhold himself. Eventually, Meyerhold wanted the actor to achieve a state of total mind–body integration. (The contrast between Stanislavski's psychological approach and Meyerhold's physical approach mirrors the split in the world of psychology occurring at about the same time, between Freud's talk therapy and Wilhelm Reich's psychophysical work.) Meyerhold's physical approach was the fountainhead of an alternative tradition that paralleled Stanislavski's and inspired various avant-garde experiments throughout the twentieth century.

A few years later, a German playwright and director, Bertolt Brecht (1898–1956), borrowed elements of both Stanislavski's and Meyerhold's methods. His theater was, like Meyerhold's, overtly theatrical, but the actors worked to create characters who were as real as those of Stanislavski. The difference was that although the character's behavior was fully rendered, the actor presented it in the spirit of a **demonstration** in order to express a judgment on it. This required the actor to maintain a slight "distance" from the character, in contrast to the absolute identification with a character demanded by Stanislavski. Brecht used his theater to promote social change by making the spectators see everyday behavior in a new light (making it seem strange) and thereby encouraging them to think about the ramifications of their own behavior and beliefs.

In the mid-twentieth century, the ideas of French actor/director Antonin Artaud (1896–1948) were especially influential in the avant-garde theater, even though Artaud never developed a specific body of technique. His four central concepts were (a) that the actor sacrifices him- or herself in the act of performing; (b) that the poetry of theater is primarily movement and sound rather than words; (c) that the actor's movement and sound have their own meanings and penetrate the spectators directly; and (d) that the resulting experience can move the spectators to a heightened state of spiritual awareness that forces them to confront their true natures.

The Polish director Jerzy Grotowski (1933–1999) used Artaud's ideas to develop a training program and body of technique based on the idea of the "Holy" actor—that is, an actor who surrenders the self totally in the act of performing. This sacrifice is achieved by rigorous physical and vocal training (called "plastique" exercises) so extreme that they break down all obstacles between impulse and expression and therefore make deception or self-censorship impossible. The authentic soul of the actor in performance becomes visible, and experiencing such a performance can encourage the audience to begin to live in a similar way.

In the social ferment in the America of the 1960s and 1970s, the influence of Meyerhold, Brecht, Artaud, and Grotowski inspired many avant-garde theaters, such as the Living Theatre created by Judith Malina and Julian Beck, the Open Theatre created by Joseph Chaikin, and the Performance Group created by Richard Schechner; political theaters, such as the Bread and Puppet Theatre created by Peter Schumann; and the longest-lived American theater, the San Francisco Mime Troupe, originally led by R. G. Davis. Each developed its own approaches to acting, but they all had several things in common. First, like Meyerhold, they were all primarily physical in their approach and stressed body and vocal work in the training of actors as well as extraordinary uses of the body and voice in performance. Second, like Artaud they were all aimed at creating theater experiences that produced powerful spiritual changes in the audience, experiences communicated primarily through physical rather than intellectual means.

Other theater makers such as Jacques Lecoq, Ariane Mnouchkine, Tadashi Suzuki, and many others have expanded on these ideas and developed approaches of their own. The evolution of the actor has continued to the present day as serious training programs have assimilated all these and many other influences, opening themselves as well to the wealth of non–Western world theater. This has produced a rich mix of philosophies and techniques in which any actor can find a place for his or her unique energies. It is a wonderful time to be an actor!

GETTING INTO THE TRADITION

An important part of your study of acting will be to immerse yourself in the living tradition of the theater, past and present. You can study the past by reading books on theater history and taking classes in it. You can keep up with current theater events by reading journals like *American Theatre Magazine,* including its online version at www.tcg.org, and visiting other interesting online sites like www.playbill.com. Newspaper articles and reviews like those in the *New York Times* (also available online) and theater columns in magazines can also help keep you up-to-date.

Most important, of course, is to see as much live theater as you can. Although there is wonderful acting to be seen in movies and television, the live stage experience is special. Being part of the living community that is a theater audience and watching the live performer has an immediacy that film performance cannot duplicate: As Orson Welles once said, "It is no accident that movies come in cans." So don't miss opportunities to attend live performances, and try to seek actors out and talk to them. One actor friend of mine says, "As an actor, I LOVE meeting students before or after shows. I have met great people in pubs from the RSC [Royal Shakespeare Company] to tiny little theatres. Actors are accessible and eager to share. Respect our time and privacy, sure, but also say hello. Cool things happen."[1] Keeping a theater journal and writing reviews can help you learn from your theater-going experiences.

> **EXERCISE 2.1: WRITING A STAGE REVIEW**
>
> As soon as possible, see a live performance and write a review of the work of one of the actors. Answer the same questions as you did in your film review: How was the actor's performance *entertaining, skillful, truthful,* and *believable within the world of the story?* How did it serve the *dramatic function* of the character? Pay special attention to the qualities of the live experience: How was it different from a film or television experience? How was the actor's performance changed by being in front of a live audience? If possible, try to meet an actor in person, and ask about his or her work.

Summary of Step 2

The long tradition of the actor has its earliest spiritual roots in the celebration of Dionysus, the Greek god of transformational life force. In the Middle Ages, the actor was an itinerant performer and a social outcast. In the Elizabethan period, the actor began to regain respectability, and the business of professional acting as we know it was reborn. Powerful actor/managers ran companies in the eighteenth century as women began to appear on stage. In the twentieth century, Stanislavski, Meyerhold, Brecht, Artaud, and others expanded the role of the actor, and this evolution has continued to the present day. An important part of your study of acting will be to immerse yourself in this living tradition of the theater, past and present.

---

[1]Actor Henry Clarke, email to the author.

STEP

3

Relaxing and Centering

A cting requires that all aspects of your being—your body, voice, thoughts, and feelings—be available, integrated, and controllable. They are the tools of your trade. As a child, you probably began life in a state of wholeness and openness, with a natural ability for engaging in fantasy and for playing with others. In the process of growing up, you may have begun to lose some of that natural wholeness and openness. There may be some aspects of your body and voice, some forms of expression, some feelings, thoughts, and experiences that you have learned to ignore or suppress. For example, touching and being touched in public may be uncomfortable for you at first. Several of the exercises that follow will require physical contact between you and your fellow students (as does the acting process itself), and if this is uncomfortable for you initially, you should share your concern privately with your teacher. Then, if you wish, you can—with your teacher's support—use your exploration of the acting process to begin overcoming physical shyness and to become more confident and comfortable in your physical identity.

The childlike qualities of wholeness and openness are necessary for an actor, and in the next three steps you will begin to rediscover them. You can recapture these qualities best when you are relaxed, playful, and nonjudgmental. Some psychologists call this the **creative state**,which is produced when your "internal parent" allows your "inner child" to come out and play. The first and most important step toward this creative state is **relaxation**, which naturally leads to greater openness and responsiveness. In a relaxed state, you will find it easy to experience what we call **centeredness**, to begin moving and sounding in a more fully integrated and controllable way, to enter into a more free and open exchange of energy with your fellow workers, and to experience the multiple levels of reality that exist simultaneously in every performance situation. These three qualities—relaxation, centeredness, and openness to others—will be the focus of the next three steps and will introduce what is, for the professional actor, the work of a lifetime of physical, vocal, mental, and spiritual development.

RELAXATION

For most of us, performing arouses anxiety. This can be both pleasurable (as in the quest for creative discovery) and unpleasant (as in the fear of failure). In either case, this anxiety can make your muscles tense and disrupt your breathing and thinking. It also interferes with your ability to react; it "freezes" you and reduces your creativity. For all these reasons, tension is the greatest enemy of the creative state. For some, **stage fright** can become so acute as to be debilitating; the great British actor Sir Laurence Olivier suffered from it so badly at one point in his career that he had to stop acting for several years.

When you find yourself scared or stuck, you may attempt to compensate by trying harder, by putting more effort into your work and trying to force your way through it. Unfortunately, this is exactly the wrong thing to do. It only increases your tension and further reduces your freedom of creative response. It is common to see student actors make the mistake of trying too hard; the harder they try, the worse they get. This excessive effort makes them more self-aware, obscures their own experience of their work, and reduces their control.

Think of trying to open a desk drawer that is stuck: If you tug at it with all your might, chances are good that it will come loose all at once and fly open, spilling the contents. Because you were using excessive force, you failed to feel the exact moment when the drawer loosened, and you lost control. You weren't experiencing the drawer anymore; you were instead experiencing only your own effort. Too often, student actors make this same mistake in performance; they stop experiencing the scene and instead become aware of their own effort, and this can become their erroneous idea of the way it feels to act.

Many actors are driven to excessive effort by their fear of failure or their desire to please their audience. They feel unworthy of the audience's attention unless they do something extraordinary to earn it; the option of doing nothing, of simply allowing themselves to "be there," is terrifying. They feel naked and exposed and become desperate to do something, anything! As a result, they have difficulty experiencing what is really happening on stage. Here is the secret that will make miracles happen for you as an actor: Acting is mostly a matter of *letting go*—letting go of too much effort, letting go of chronic physical tension, letting go of a false voice, letting go of your preconceptions about the work, letting go of fear, and, most of all, letting go of who you already are in order to become someone new.

The first step in letting go is *relaxation*. For an actor, relaxation does not mean reduced energy or slackness; rather it means that all unnecessary tensions have been removed, the remaining energy has been purposefully focused, and awareness is at a high level. The kind of relaxation you want is a state in which you are most ready to react to the slightest stimulus, like the cat in front of the mouse hole. Although the cat is completely alert and in total readiness to spring, it is not tense. If it were tense, the tension in its muscles would slow down its reactions and make its movements awkward, and it would miss the mouse. The same is true of people.

The best description of the relaxed actor's state is what meditators call *restful alertness*. You are already capable of restful alertness; you don't need to do anything to achieve it but only to become still enough to experience it. Do this now, through a simple meditation.

EXERCISE 3.1: A MEDITATION

Sit comfortably in your chair, both feet flat on the floor, back and neck straight but not rigid, hands resting on your thighs. Look at a spot on the floor eight feet in front of you, or if you like, close your eyes. Focus your awareness on your breath flowing in and out of your nose. Allow any thoughts that come up to play across your consciousness, and then simply return your awareness to your breath. Resist nothing. Sit for as long as you are comfortable. Whatever experience you have is correct.

The ability to relax can be learned. Psychologists speak of the "relaxation response," which develops with repetition just like any other skill. The following exercise is a classic in the field of relaxation. Although you can quickly learn it on your own, it would be useful for your teacher or a partner to lead you at first so you aren't distracted by having to read the instructions. If necessary, a tape recording of these instructions with the necessary pauses could guide you.

EXERCISE 3.2: PHASIC RELAXATION

Lie in a comfortable position, knees slightly raised and feet flat on the floor. As in your meditation, your breath is the focus of your awareness. Imagine that each inhalation is a warm, energy-filled fluid flowing into your body. Each exhalation carries away with it tension and inhibition, like a refreshing outgoing wave. Breathe deeply and easily in a slow, natural, regular rhythm.

Each successive breath will be sent into a different part of the body. As the breath flows into each area, let the muscles there tighten as much as they can; then, as the breath flows out, let the muscles release as the breath carries all the tension away with it, leaving the area refreshed and at ease. Exhaling is letting go.

The sequence of breaths moves from the top of the body to the feet. Increasingly, the regular rhythm of your breathing should make the muscular contractions and relaxations flow smoothly down the body like a slow wave. Send your breath into each of these areas in turn:

1. The *forehead and scalp*—furrowing your brow and then releasing it; keeping your eyes at rest, closed and turned slightly downward.

2. The *jaw*—clenching it and then letting it fall easily downward until your teeth are about one-half inch apart.
3. The *tongue*—extending it and then letting it lie easily in your mouth.
4. The *front of the neck*—extending your chin down to touch your chest, stretching the back of the neck, and then rolling your head easily back.
5. The *back of the neck*—rolling the top of your head back and under to touch the floor, stretching the front of your neck, and then rolling your head slowly back down so that the neck is longer than before.
6. The *upper chest*—swelling your chest outward in all directions so that the shoulders are widened; then letting your chest easily subside so that you feel your shoulder blades spread, wider than before.
7. The *arms and hands*—letting them become stiff and straight like steel rods, clenching your hands into fists, and then letting your hands uncurl and your arms melt into the floor.
8. The *pit of the stomach*—clenching it into a small, hard ball, and then, with a sigh, releasing it.
9. The *legs and knees*—stiffening your knees as you straighten your legs, pushing your feet downward, and then releasing your legs and feeling them melt into the floor.
10. The *feet*—with the backs of your heels still touching the floor, stretching your toes up toward your chin, and then releasing them, letting them fall into a natural position.
11. The *length of the body*—pushing the backs of your heels and your shoulder blades simultaneously downward into the floor so that your whole body lifts upward in a long arch, and then, with a sigh, letting your body slowly fall, lengthening as it relaxes and melting deep into the floor.

Now take ten deep, slow, regular breaths, and with each breath move more deeply into relaxation, as you remain alert and refreshed. The flow of breath is a continuous cycle of energy that is stored comfortably in the body; with each breath, this store of energy is increased. If a yawn comes to you, enjoy it fully, and vocalize the exhalation, letting the sound of the yawn pour out.

As you repeat this exercise on successive days, you can give yourself the instructions silently. Keep a steady rhythm that follows the tempo of your deep, relaxed breathing. Gradually, the action of the exercise will become natural, and you will no longer need to think of the instructions, giving your full awareness to the flow of contractions and relaxations that follow your breath as it travels down your body like a wave—awakening, refreshing, and relaxing your body and making you ready for work. Use this exercise as an easy and quick preparation for all future work. Over a period of time, it will help break up and dissolve chronic bundles of tension within your body. Like any skill, relaxation must be developed over a period of time and maintained once achieved. Meditation and relaxation techniques are used by many actors throughout their lives.

FINDING THE CENTER

In addition to learning to relax, you must also develop *wholeness*. Good acting requires that all the parts of your body, your voice, and your mind work together in an integrated way. This integration is a natural state. Even if, as you've grown up, you have learned habits of movement or voice that have made you unintegrated and awkward, you can easily rediscover your natural wholeness. You begin by experiencing the true source of integrated movement and voice deep in the center of your body.

This idea of a personal center is not just a metaphor, it has a tangible physical dimension. There is a "pure" center deep within your body, at your center of gravity, roughly three finger-widths below your navel. It is here that the breath (and therefore the voice) originates, as well as all large motions of the body. Golfers, baseball players, and many other kinds of athletes learn to initiate movement from this center, and so must the actor. The pure center is the undistorted source from which our work begins in order to develop the unique ways of using the body and voice required by whatever character we will create throughout the rest of our working process. Here is an exercise to help you develop a specific sense of your physical center.

EXERCISE 3.3: FINDING YOUR CENTER

Stand upright and relax. Clear your mind and witness your body as it performs the following activities:

1. Move either foot out to the side about two feet; then rock from foot to foot, feeling your center of gravity moving from side to side. Quickly make your rocking motions smaller and smaller, like a bowling pin that almost falls down. Come to rest on center.
2. Move either foot forward about two feet; make front-to-back rocking motions, and again come to rest on center.
3. Move your center around rotationally, exploring the limits of various stances. Feel the weight of your body flowing out of your center, through your legs, and into the ground.
4. With one finger, point at the spot in your body that you feel is your center; don't be concerned about where it ought to be, but sense where it really is.
5. Explore how your center is involved in breathing, making sound, and moving.

In this exercise, you may have found that your center is not at the "pure" location just below your navel. Many of us have lost touch with this natural center and operate instead from some higher center, such as our chests, or even our heads. Unfortunately, when we fail to work from our pure center, we inevitably look and sound stiff and superficial, and our movements and voice will not have the fullness and expressiveness needed for performance. You may need to repeat this exercise over a period of days and weeks, letting your sense of center drop until the pure center starts to feel natural to you.

Cicely Berry, Voice Director of the Royal Shakespeare Company, says that the center is where laughter begins. Developing your sense of a physical center will help you to develop a psychological and spiritual centeredness as well, because at this deep level your energy exists simultaneously in physical, psychological, and spiritual forms.

As you become aware of your center over a period of days, you will notice that it moves within your body as your mood changes; frequently, your center will rise upward when you are in an excited or fearful state, or downward in states of well-being or determination. You will notice, too, that different people have different characteristic centers and that the locations of their centers are very appropriate to their personalities. Such diversity can be found in people who have a "lot of guts" or who "follow their noses," "lead with their chins," are "all heart," "drag their feet," "have their heads in the clouds," and so on. Although we begin our work from our ideal center, there is no "correct" voice or posture for a performance until these are determined by the demands of the role.

Summary of Step 3

For most of us, performing arouses anxiety. This makes us tense, interferes with our ability to react, and reduces our creativity. For all these reasons, tension is the greatest enemy of the creative state, and the first step toward that creative state is to relax. When we speak of relaxation for an actor, we do not mean the ordinary sense of reduced energy or slackness, but rather a state in which all unnecessary tensions have been removed, energy has been purposefully focused, and awareness is at a high level. This is what meditators call "restful alertness."

Besides being relaxed, actors also need to be whole, because good acting requires that all the parts of the body, voice, and mind work together in an integrated way. The true source of integrated movement and voice is deep within the center of the body, roughly three finger-widths below the navel. It is here that breath (and therefore voice), as well as laughter, all large motions of the body, and all the deepest impulses originate. The pure center is an undistorted source from which to begin our work and develop in any way required by a role. Eventually, we will find the center appropriate to the character.

4

Breathing, Sounding, and Moving from the Center

The relaxation exercise (3.2) focused on breath for a very good reason: Breath is life. The word *psychology* means "study of the soul," and the word for soul, *psyche,* originally meant "vital breath." Think about it: When you breathe, you are bringing the outside world into your body and then sending it out again. Your breath constantly reflects your relationship to your world. When you are frightened, you hold your breath because you don't want to let the threatening world in. When you are happy, your breath flows freely. The way you feel about your world is expressed in the way you breathe it in and breathe it out.

For this reason your natural voice, which is based on your breath, expresses your inner state. Speaking—as well as sobbing, laughing, gasping, sighing, and all the other sounds you make—is the natural and automatic reflection of your relationship to your world. Your voice so completely reflects your inner state that the act of speaking or sounding *turns you inside out.*

Consequently, actors are careful not to force their voices into unnatural and artificial patterns and often work hard to free their natural voices from bad habits. Unfortunately, the influence of television has turned many of us into "talking heads," causing us to lose touch with the natural breathing that begins deep inside our bodies. Here is an exercise that will help you to experience the natural integration of breath, body, and voice.

EXERCISE 4.1: BREATHING AND SOUNDING FROM YOUR CENTER

1. Sit comfortably in your chair, or lie on the floor. Relax yourself by allowing your breath to sweep through your body as in the relaxation exercise (3.2). As you breathe easily and slowly, become aware that your breath is rising and falling from a deep place in your body, a little below your navel.

2. As your breath travels outward from this deep place, make sound lightly; do not disturb your breath, just allow it to vibrate, as it may sometimes do just as you are falling asleep. This is your natural voice—your vibrating breath carrying energy from deep within you into the outside world.

3. Reach effortlessly with your vibrating breath into the world around you. Put yourself, randomly, into new positions, and experience the vibrating breath flowing through each. What changes occur in your voice?

4. As you continue to produce sound, feel the vibrations of that sound spreading into every part of your body: out of the neck and into the head and chest; into the back, the stomach, the buttocks; into the arms and hands; into the legs and feet; and into the scalp. Feel the sound radiating from every part of your body. With the touch of a light fingertip, check every surface of your body. Are there "dead spots" that are not participating in the sound?

Examine your experience during sounding: Did you have a new sense of the capacity of your entire body to join in the act of sounding? Did you feel more in touch with yourself and with the space around you, as if your sound were literally reaching outside yourself in a tangible way? Are you now more alert, refreshed, and relaxed? You have begun to experience how physical, vocal, and mental qualities are integral to one another, because the body, voice, and mind are all integral to one another, and breath is the great unifier that binds them all together.

THE CYCLE OF ENERGY

Whenever we try to do something, to achieve some objective—that is, whenever we *act*—we send energy flowing out from our centers into the outer world in the form of sound, speech, gesture, or movement. Usually, our action provokes a reaction from someone, and we receive the new energy of this reaction through seeing, hearing, or touching. This new energy flows into us and touches our center, which in turn elicits a further reaction from us, and so on. It is this flow of energy from character to character through the chain of action and reaction (i.e., cause and effect) that makes a play unfold. We will call each exchange of action and reaction an **interaction**.

This idea of a cycle of energy is central to Asian martial arts such as *tai chi chuan,* and study in these arts can be of great benefit to an actor. Here is an exercise taken from yoga that will let you experience the cycle of energy (see Figure 4.1).

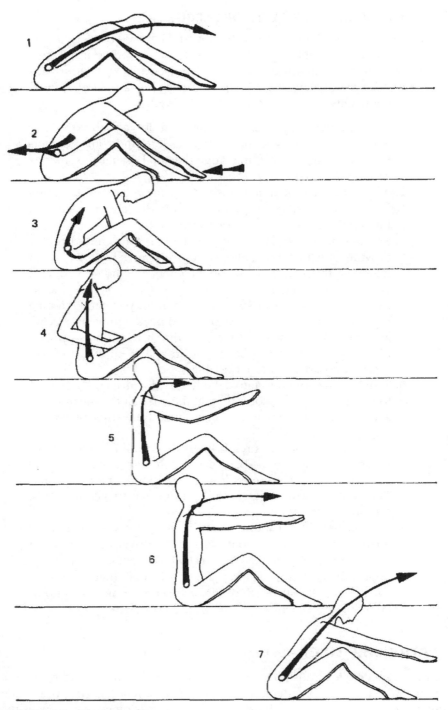

FIGURE 4.1   The cycle of Energy.

EXERCISE 4.2: YOUR CYCLE OF ENERGY

Sit on the floor with your back straight, and spread your legs a little with the knees slightly raised. Feel as if you are being lifted from your center and out through the top of your head so that your back and neck are long and wide. Keep your head level, your eyes looking straight ahead, and your waist level as well.

1. As you breathe out, reach forward and down with your arms and torso, keeping your back and neck long and your shoulders wide. Imagine yourself in a large theater, bowing to someone sitting in the last row.
2. As you begin to breathe in, use your arms and hands to gather your breath into the lower part of your body, scooping "energy" into the funnel formed by your legs.
3. As your breath begins to fill you, feel its warmth and power flowing up within you. Follow its upward movement with your hands, so that your arms scoop the energy in and upward as if you are embracing it.
4. As your breath rises in your body, let it lift you, straightening and lengthening your upper torso and neck, lifting your head, and widening your shoulders and throat as it flows upward like a wave moving through you in a slow undulation. Let yourself unfurl like a fern opening.
5. That breath then flows into the outer world; give an "ah" sound to that imaginary person sitting at the back of the theater, and accompany it with an unfolding gesture of the arms toward the person.
6. As the power of that breath begins to diminish, close your mouth so the "ah" sound becomes an "oh" and then an "m," and experience a tingling sensation in your mouth and nose areas. The smooth flow of the sound produces a trisyllable word, "ah-oh-m," or *om*.
7. As your breath and sound die away, let your body again bow forward and down and your arms reach forward to scoop in a new quantity of breath energy, as the cycle begins again.
8. Repeat the cycle several times, feeling the continuity of inward and outward breaths so the entire exercise becomes one unbroken, flowing experience with no sharp corners.

RELATIONSHIP TO GRAVITY

You live in specific relationship to gravity, and you move and sound within that relationship. Like your breathing, the way you experience gravity is a fundamental expression of your relationship to your world. Some days it seems that you wake up heavier, with "the weight of the world" on your shoulders, and you feel "down"; at the saddest times you say you have a "heavy heart." On the other hand, sometimes you feel "up" or "light-hearted." When you are sure of yourself, you feel as if you are receiving strength from gravity, and you speak of "knowing where I stand" or "holding my ground."

People's attitudes toward gravity can be seen in their postures. When Arthur Miller opens his play *Death of a Salesman* with Willy Loman crossing the stage, back bent under the weight of his sample case, Willy's sense of defeat and hopelessness is directly expressed in the way he is losing his fight with gravity. In musical theater, in contrast, it is a convention that lovers actually defy gravity by skipping, as if they were about to float away "on cloud nine." Here is an exercise to help you discover the various ways in which you experience gravity.

EXERCISE 4.3: ROOTS

Imagine yourself standing on a mirror; below you is your other self with its own center. Imagine a bond between your center "up here" and the one "down there" in your mirror image. This imaginary bond of energy is like a root. As you move, your root moves with you; you can even "detach" your root. Try the following movements, but don't act them out; simply experience them through these images, and discover what they feel like.

1. Select a destination; detach and lift your root, move to the destination, and replant your root there.
2. Now move to a destination without lifting your root, plowing a furrow through the ground as you move. Feel yourself pushing your whole body through space. We will call this *molding*.
3. Now lift your root, and leave it dangling the whole time, whether moving or standing still. We will call this *floating*.
4. Now imagine the root being drawn upward, still attached at your center, but lifting your center upward and out through the top of your head. Move with the sense that you have to reach down to touch the floor; you are *flying*.

There are distinct differences among the experiences of molding, floating, and flying, and each of them might express several different things: Molding, for instance, can feel like dejection or defeat, but it might also feel like determination or commitment; floating can feel like joy or enthusiasm, but it might also feel like confusion or vulnerability. The particular emotional quality of any one of these states is determined only by the context of the play.

Begin to observe in everyday life how the position of people's bodily centers and their relationships to gravity express their characters and moods. You might even record your observations in an acting journal, noting expressive postures, gestures, and utterances you observe in daily life. Many actors find a journal useful not only to record such observations, but also to record experiences and ideas that result from their work as actors.

PHRASING MOVEMENT

In the previous exercise you began to move through space by "lifting" your rooted center, moving, and then "planting" your rooted center again at your destination. Review this experience: Did it give you a heightened sense of clarity and purposefulness in your movements? Did the exercise make you more aware of the *shape* of your movements?

Stanislavski said that "everything that happens on a stage should have a definite purpose," and this includes stage movement. When an actor moves on stage, he or she is moving for a definite purpose; that movement is driven by some objective that is usually in relation to other characters. For example, he or she may be approaching other characters, either in a positive way (such as persuading, imploring, or embracing them) or a negative way (such as threatening or attacking them). Alternatively, the actor may be avoiding or retreating from other characters in fear or disgust or respect. Whatever the quality of the movement, it is an active expression of action and relationship.

You will find that when you are in action, you will naturally feel impulses to move appropriately to your action, and these impulses generate what we call the **blocking** of the scene. Blocking is the physical form of the action of the scene expressed in changing spatial relationships between the characters and their environment (more on this in Step 15).

Whatever causes it, good stage movement must have clarity and well-defined shape. In good writing or speaking, thoughts are shaped into phrases and sentences, each with a clear shape that is essential to good communication. In the same way, your stage movement needs to be organized and shaped into clear phraseology.

EXERCISE 4.4: PHRASING MOVEMENT

As in Exercise 4.3, begin by "seeing" your own rooted center in relationship to your mirror image beneath the floor. Now make a movement by following each of these steps:

1. Think of a specific destination.
2. Begin to move by lifting the root; exaggerate this motion at first.
3. Carry your root to your destination, and "land" there.
4. As you land, "spear" your root into the floor to complete your movement.
5. Repeat this action several times, paying special attention to the sense of beginning, middle, and end with each movement phrase.
6. Now begin to play with variations of this cycle, extending them beyond realistic movement. For instance, try lifting the root slowly and heavily, and then drag it to the destination and dump it there so that it "plops" into the ground. Or make your lift light and high, moving away from your destination, and then throw your root toward your destination and fly there,

landing with a light jump. Invent other patterns and qualities of movement but in each case keep a clear sense of the beginning, middle, and end of each movement.

Notice also that when you are *not* moving, you are grounded and still. Avoid wandering unless it is appropriate to your action (for instance, if your character is confused and desperate) although even this must be expressed in a clear and purposeful way. Beginning actors often have difficulty standing still; they tend to rock from foot to foot or wander aimlessly. This is a natural expression of uncertainty, discomfort, and a lack of clear purpose on the stage. Conversely, some beginning actors manifest their anxiety by "locking up" so rigidly that they are unable to react readily. Avoid both extremes. Learn to stand still, and yet be ready to move. When you do move, make your movements economical and purposeful, clearly shaped with a beginning, middle, and end.

Summary of Step 4

When you breathe, you are bringing the outside world into your body and then sending it out again. Your breath constantly reflects your relationship to your world. Your natural voice, originating in your breath, is the way you turn yourself inside out.

You experience your center in specific relationship to gravity, and you move and sound within that relationship. Consequently, the way you experience gravity is also a fundamental expression of your relationship to your world. Three of the ways we experience gravity are called molding, floating, and flying.

Stage movement is a physical expression of action. It must be clearly shaped—with the same kind of phraseology that any good expression has and with a clear beginning, middle, and end.

5 Collaboration

Actors always collaborate, literally "labor together" with others, whether in a stage play, TV show, or film. They work not only with other actors, but also with directors, stage managers, costume and makeup people, and many others. The success of any collaborative artistic endeavor depends on the ability of these many kinds of artists to work together toward the common goal of bringing the material to life.

When a group works together in the best possible way, the energy of each member of the group flows into a common stream, forming one energy that is greater than the sum of its parts. Everyone on the team receives more energy from the group than he or she gives to it. No member of the team needs to sacrifice individuality; rather, each member finds his or her individual power enhanced by membership in the group.

Such ideal teamwork is achieved when five conditions have been met:

1. Each member is genuinely *committed* to being a member of the team.
2. Each member *supports* the work of the others.
3. There is *trust* and *mutual respect* within the team.
4. All members agree to maintain free and open *communication*.
5. The efforts of all members are *aligned* with the common purpose.

Let's examine each of these points.

Commitment. It is part of your responsibility as an actor to be committed on five levels at once:

To *your own talent*—being as good as you can be and continually striving to be better

To each *role* you play—finding the truth of the character and of each moment in the performance

To each *ensemble* of which you are a member—contributing to the success and growth of everyone in it

To each piece of *material* you perform—finding and expressing the truth it contains

To your *audience* and the *world* you serve through your work.

Support for Your Partners. We all have different reasons for working in the theater or film, but we support each other's objectives, even if we do not share them. We assume a nonjudgmental attitude.

Trust and Mutual Respect. We respect other workers as a matter of principle; we treat them exactly as we would want to be treated ourselves. We trust all of our partners to do their jobs, and even if we disagree with their methods, we do our best to accept and utilize their contributions. If this eventually proves to be impossible, we seek resolution through respectful but honest and direct communication.

Free and Open Communication. No matter how supportive, trustful, and respectful we all are, creative collaboration is difficult, and we are bound to encounter differences of opinion, conflicting needs, and artistic challenges. All these problems can become opportunities for creativity as long as we can communicate freely and reasonably about them.

Alignment. When every member of the team shares a common purpose, each is free to work in his or her own way and still contribute to the overall effort. People with very different artistic methods—as well as different political, religious, cultural, and artistic values—can work in alignment toward a common purpose as long as the common purpose is well understood by all and the other four conditions listed here have been met.

Commitment, support, trust and respect, communication, and *alignment*—these are the cornerstones of teamwork, and they all require that you keep your attention on the job at hand and *park your ego at the rehearsal room door.* Here are four enjoyable exercises that explore these qualities on a literal, physical level.

EXERCISE 5.1: FALLING

1. After everybody picks a partner, stand three feet behind your partner, keeping one foot back for stability (see Figure 5.1). By mutual agreement, your partner will start to fall backward, keeping his or her body straight but not stiff. Catch your partner right away, and gently raise him or her back up.
2. Repeat the exercise, allowing your partner to fall gradually farther and farther, until he or she falls to about four feet above the floor. If your partner becomes frightened, reassure him or her.
3. Reverse roles and repeat.

Caution: Do not attempt this exercise unless you are confident of being able to catch your partner; otherwise, serious injury could result.

FIGURE 5.1   Falling Exercise.

EXERCISE 5.2: FLOATING

1. Form groups of seven or nine with one person becoming the "floater." The floaters lie flat on the floor, close their eyes, and fold their arms across their chests. The others kneel beside them, three or four on either side, and prepare to lift them (see Figure 5.2A).
2. Everyone begins to breathe in unison. When the breathing rhythm is established, the group *gently and slowly* lifts the floater, keeping him or her perfectly level. Those being lifted should feel as if they are floating.
3. Lift the floater as high as possible while still keeping him or her level (see Figure 5.2B).
4. Slowly lower the floater, rocking him or her gently back and forth, like a leaf settling to earth.
5. Repeat with each member of the group.

Now let's use our collaborative skills to create a group scene.

EXERCISE 5.3: TUG OF WAR

1. Each member of the group creates—in pantomime—a piece of rope about two feet long.
2. Standing in a single long line, each member "attaches" his or her rope to the pieces on either side, creating one long rope.
3. The two people at the center move apart so that the group is divided into two teams.
4. Have a tug of war, but don't let the rope stretch or break. Continue until one team wins.

This exercise is a good example of performance reality: The rope ceases to be real if any member of the group fails to make his or her part real and

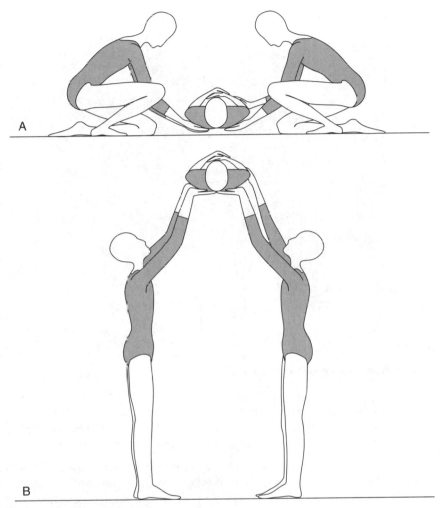

FIGURE 5.2   Floating Exercise.

connected to the whole. *Every individual actor must believe in the whole rope.* This explains why we say that "there are no small parts, only small actors." The total reality of the show depends on the completeness of every element in it.

EXERCISE 5.4: GROUP LEVITATION

1. Stand in one large, perfectly round circle, facing inward. All participants put their arms around the waists of the persons on either side (see Figure 5.3).

2. Start to breathe in unison. Bend your knees slightly when exhaling, and lift the person on either side as you breathe in. Do not lift yourself; lift those you are holding, and allow yourself to be lifted by them.

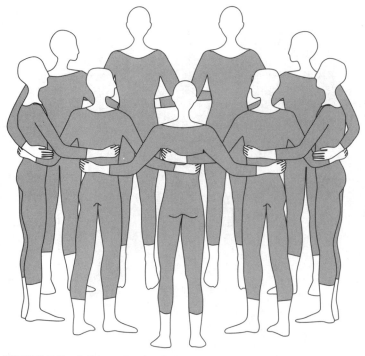

FIGURE 5.3   A Group Levitation.

   3. As you breathe out, say the word *higher*, and try to lift those
   you are holding higher and higher. Allow the rhythm of the
   group to accelerate naturally until you all *leave the ground*.

   Do you see how this exercise symbolizes the way we work together? When
the energy of every member of the group is connected to the common goal and
there is a basis of mutual trust, respect, and open communication, the result is
greater than the sum of its parts: Everyone gets more energy back than he or
she gives!

LEADING AND FOLLOWING

When an ensemble is functioning well, energy flows easily among all the members. The roles of leader and follower are constantly changing so smoothly that
it is difficult to say at any moment who is a leader and who is a follower; rather,
it seems that everyone is leading and following at once. The following exercises
will give you the experience of this simultaneous leading and following.

EXERCISE 5.5: LEADING AND FOLLOWING

   1. *Blind leading.* You and your partner lightly interlace your fin-
   gertips up to the first joint. Your partner closes his or her eyes,
   and you silently lead him or her around the room. As you gain

confidence and control, you can begin to move faster and extend the range of your travels. Soon you can run! If your situation permits, you can even take a trip to some distant destination. Then you can reverse roles and repeat for the trip back.

2. *Sound leading.* Begin as in #1, but when you are well under way, break physical contact and begin to lead your partner by repeating a single word, which your partner follows by sound alone. Again, extend your range and speed. Run! *Caution: Be prepared to grab your partner to prevent a collision.*

Review the experience of this exercise. As a follower, did you trust your partner enough to truly commit your weight to your movement? As a leader, did you receive your partner's energy and respond to his or her momentum? Let's continue with another exercise to explore simultaneous leading and following.

EXERCISE 5.6: MIRRORS

1. You and a partner decide who is A and who is B. Stand facing each other. Person A makes slow "underwater" movements that B can mirror completely. Try to keep the partnership moving in unison. The movements should flow in a continually changing stream, avoiding repeated patterns. Bigger, more continuous movements are easier to follow.

2. At a signal, the roles are instantly reversed *without a break in the action.* B is now the leader; A is the follower. Continue moving from the deep centers of your bodies; feel yourselves beginning to share a common center through your shared movement, from which come a common breathing and a common sound that arise naturally from your movement.

3. The roles are reversed a few more times; each time the leadership role changes, the movement and sound continue without interruption.

4. Finally, there is no leader. Neither A nor B leads, but you and your partner continue to move and sound together.

Watch other partnerships doing this exercise: Do you see how intense and connected to each other they seem? Our listening to and seeing each other in performance should always have this kind of intensity; you will be leading and following others during a scene just as much as you did in these exercises. Here's another exercise exploring this through sound (see Figure 5.4).

EXERCISE 5.7: COOKIE SEARCH

1. Everyone in the group chooses a partner. Then the entire group stands together in a clump at the center of the room with eyes closed. Then all spin around a few times until no one knows which way he or she is facing.

2. Without opening your eyes, move slowly in whatever direction you are facing until you reach a wall or other obstacle. Avoid

FIGURE 5.4   A Cookie Search.

touching anyone else; feel your way with all of your nonvisual senses.

3. When you have gone as far as you can (and still have not opened your eyes), begin to search for your partner using only the word *cookie.*

4. When you find each other, open your eyes and wait in silence for all to finish. Enjoy watching the others search. Feel the drama of the exercise.

In this exercise you were not led but had to find your own way toward the sounds of your partner. Did you feel lonely while searching for your partner and relieved when you found him or her? Don't be the kind of actor who makes partners feel lonely during a performance!

SEEING AND HEARING

On stage or screen, a good story moves toward a dramatic conclusion as *energy passes from character to character through a series of interactions that form the scenes of the play* (more on this crucial idea later). The continuity and strength of this flow of energy are what give the story its momentum, which in acting we call **pace**. If the flow is interrupted for any reason, the momentum is broken, and the evolving drama stalls, causing a drop in dramatic tension and suspense.

Actors usually focus their attention on the energy they *send* to another actor as they pursue their objectives through the actions of their characters (again, more on this in later steps). It is equally important, however, that each actor *receive* the energy from the other actors, which provokes each action; as we say, *acting is reacting*. If actors react only to their premeditated ideas of what they are "supposed" to be receiving from another actor, instead of what they are really receiving here and now, the flow of the scene will not be a real event.

Actors receive energy, of course, through seeing and hearing one another. Moreover, drama involves circumstances in which the stakes are raised and what the characters get from one another has special significance; seeing and hearing on stage must therefore be more acute than in real life.

One way to experience such heightened perception is to think of yourself as a camera that is recording everything you see and hear on stage. This is not just a metaphor; an audience does, in fact, tend to mimic the seeing and hearing of the actor. When you focus intently on a particular detail on stage, for example, audience members feel as if they are seeing that detail in a close-up. You act as a virtual camera for your audience. Here is an enjoyable exercise that will give you the experience of this kind of significant seeing and hearing.

EXERCISE 5.8: CAMERA GAME

Choose some simple activity that you can do with a partner, such as playing a game of cards, preparing a meal, bowling, or playing tennis. You and your partner should take turns being the "camera." Whoever is the camera should take the most interesting pictures possible; you are free to move in any way the camera might move, zooming in for close-ups, panning across the scene, cutting from one angle to another, and so on. When your teacher or your partner randomly calls out "Switch," you will instantly switch roles between camera and subject.

After the exercise, discuss the scene. Was your hearing and seeing of one another heightened? Did being the camera give you greater freedom from self-awareness? Were you more active as the camera? Do you see why having a meaningful and active objective (in this case taking pictures) is so effective on stage?

GETTING AND GIVING NOTES

Throughout your work as an actor, both in class and in rehearsal, you will depend on the feedback you get about your work from others. When feedback is given in a formal way, as in a classroom critique or during a rehearsal, it is called giving *notes*. But whether the feedback is formal or not, actors depend on it more than most other artists do; the comments you get from your teachers, directors, and fellow actors are tremendously important in guiding your development as an actor and the creation of a specific role. Therefore, actors and directors have a solemn responsibility to provide accurate and useful feedback to one another. Many of the remaining exercises in this book require you to discuss your work and the work of others. Use these principles for effective communication:

1. Don't guess what is going on inside someone else; instead, say what you *see* and how it makes you *feel*. Don't say, "Why are you hiding?" Say, "I noticed that you rarely looked at your partner during this scene, and that made me feel as if you were hiding."
2. Take the time to be *clear* about your message before you deliver it.
3. Be *specific, simple,* and *direct*.
4. Above all, remember that our aim is to support and respect one another and the work itself. Be objective—keep your focus on the work and off personalities.

Summary of Step 5

Actors always work in a group situation. The success of the process depends on the ability of everyone to work together toward the common goal of bringing the material to life. When a group works together in the best possible way, the energy of each member of the group flows into a common stream, forming one energy that is greater than the sum of its parts. Such ideal teamwork is achieved only when five conditions have been met: First, each member is genuinely committed to being a member of the team; second, each member supports the work of the others; third, that support is founded on trust and mutual respect; fourth, all agree to maintain free and open communication; and fifth, the efforts of each member are aligned with the common purpose. When all these conditions have been met, each member of the group is empowered to do his or her best work, and each gets more energy from the group than he or she gives to it.

The connection between actors, through which the energy of the scene flows, depends on the ability of each actor to lead and to follow simultaneously, and to give and receive through significant hearing, seeing, and touching. The real interactions between actors, when created in this way, provide a strong focus of attention that helps to reduce self-awareness and thereby promotes creativity.

Good communication between actors and directors is essential and is best when it is clear, simple, direct, and objective.

Summary of Part One

The actor's job is to fulfill the dramatic purpose of a role in a believable, skillful, and truthful way and to use his or her power over the lives of the audience in an ethically responsible way.

The long tradition of the actor has its earliest spiritual roots in the celebration of Dionysus, the Greek god of transformational life force. In the Middle Ages, the actor was an itinerant performer and a social outcast. In the Elizabethan period, the actor began to regain respectability, and the business of professional acting as we know it was reborn. Powerful actor/managers ran companies in the eighteenth century as women began to appear on stage. In the twentieth century, Stanislavski, Meyerhold, Brecht, Artaud, and others expanded the role of the actor, and this evolution has continued to the present day.

The creative state requires playfulness and relaxation; tension and excessive effort disrupt our ability to react and invent. The actor must learn to let go of premeditations and physical tension and enter into a state of purposeful relaxation, which can be called restful alertness. In this relaxed state, you learn to operate from the deep center of your body. Working from this undistorted center gives you unity and rhythm; you then experiment to find the center and quality of energy appropriate to a role.

Your breath, voice, and large movements originate in your deep center. Your energy travels toward the outside world as breath, sound, or movement, all of which reflect your inner world. Operating in this way, you turn yourself inside out as energy flows out of you and provokes a reaction in the outside world, which you then receive. This cycle of giving and receiving forms the interactions that move the story of a play forward.

All of this is experienced within the field of gravity, and your relationship to gravity is a fundamental expression of your relationship to the world. Entering into a character's action can inspire in you an experience of gravity, a center, and a quality of energy that are fundamental and unique to the role.

For the actor, this process of discovery always occurs within a group context. Teamwork is best achieved when everyone is committed, supportive, trustful and respectful, open, and aligned with the common purpose. When these conditions are met, all members of the group receive more energy from the group than they give to it, and the whole becomes greater than the sum of its parts.

PART TWO

Discovering Action

Consider the word *actor*. At its root, it means "someone who acts," who *does* something. Think for a moment: Why do you do things in everyday life? Usually, it is to get something you want or need. Sometimes what you need is related to physical survival: food, money, or shelter. Sometimes your need is emotional: to be understood, to be loved, to find peace or beauty. Whatever your need, if it is urgent enough, you *do* something about it. You *act* in order to achieve some **objective** that you hope will satisfy your **need**.

Characters in plays, TV shows, and movies are shown in situations in which something important is happening. In such dramatic situations, whether funny or sad, the needs of the characters are heightened; they are compelled to try to satisfy their needs by doing often-extraordinary things. This is what makes the story interesting to us; we can feel ourselves in the place of the characters because we also try to do things to fulfill our needs every day, though not usually in such extraordinary ways or circumstances. We feel **suspense** as we wait to see whether the characters will get what they need or not. Will Oedipus find the killer of Laius? Will Romeo and Juliet get together? Will Spiderman save the world?

This basic definition of acting is at the heart of everything in this book: *Immediate and urgent needs cause actions in the pursuit of objectives within given circumstances.* This is a complex idea; read it aloud several times, and become aware of each of its four elements: *needs, actions, objectives,* and *circumstances*. We will explore each of these elements in the following steps.

This view of acting as "doing" rather than "showing" or "telling about" is the single most important and profound concept in the contemporary view of the actor's art. It is summed up by the term

action, and you cannot understand the modern idea of acting without understanding the idea of action.

EXAMPLE PLAYS

As the remaining steps examine each component of the acting process, I will provide examples taken from five sources: Arthur Miller's *Death of a Salesman,* Tennessee Williams's *The Glass Menagerie,* Lorraine Hansberry's *A Raisin in the Sun*, Luis Valdez's *Zoot Suit,* and an episode of the television show *Cheers* by Tom Reeder. I will also refer in passing to Shakespeare's *Hamlet* and Samuel Beckett's *Endgame.*

My examples will be much more useful to you if you read these plays in their entirety at the outset. They are available in libraries and bookstores, in paperback, and in many anthologies; the script for the *Cheers* episode is available in Appendix A at the back of this book. All the plays were also produced as feature films and are available on video. The best of several film versions of *The Glass Menagerie*, made in 1987, was directed by Paul Newman and starred Joanne Woodward and John Malkovich. *A Raisin in the Sun* was filmed in 1961 and starred Sidney Poitier, Ruby Dee, and Claudia McNeil. (A 1989 version with Danny Glover and Esther Rolle gives a good sense of how the play lived on stage.) *Zoot Suit*, produced in 1981 and starring Edward James Olmos, was filmed entirely in the theater where it was first performed. Watching any of these films will enhance the experience of reading the play but will not substitute for it.

6   Actions and Objectives

We can go all the way back to 350 BCE and Aristotle's *Poetics,* the very first writing about Western drama, to begin understanding the concept of action. The main difference between drama and other kinds of writing, Aristotle said, is that drama shows us a thing happening *as if before our eyes* and *for the first time.* Other kinds of writing can tell us a story and may even contain dramatic elements, but a play presents the story as something happening right now, right here. A play is not "about" something; it "is" the event itself.

In the same way, the good actor's performance is not "about" the character; it "is" the character living before our eyes as if for the first time. Consequently, we say that acting is *doing,* not showing or telling. Like the play itself, the actor has to be here and now, doing the thing itself as if for the first time, *in action.*

Action is expressed in many ways: physical, vocal, intellectual, emotional, and spiritual. When an actor is truly in action, all these aspects of the performance combine into one unified state and become interconnected: An adjustment in the body can generate a change of emotion, a change in the voice can generate new thoughts and emotions, a new emotional experience can generate physical and vocal changes, and so on. Acting can be approached in all of these ways, and the best actor training programs simultaneously address them all.

This explains why so many different acting techniques can all produce good results, though one or another may be more effective for an individual actor. Whether they approach acting primarily through the body and voice, the mind, the emotions, or the spirit, all contemporary acting techniques are aimed at creating a dynamic actor who does things in a total, authentic, and dramatically effective way, rather than an actor who merely shows off or shows us an image or idea of the character instead of the living character in action.

STANISLAVSKI'S VIEW OF ACTION

Constantin Stanislavski was one of the first to explore the idea of action in a systematic way. He was dissatisfied with the overblown acting style of his time; too often, he felt, the actor's display of emotion and technique became an end in itself and overshadowed the meaning of the play. Stanislavski set out to create a new system of acting aimed at economy, greater psychological truthfulness, and, above all, respect for the ideas of the play. He based his system on the idea that everything an actor does in a performance has to be **justified** by the character's internal need. As Stanislavski said:

> There are no physical actions divorced from some desire, some effort in some direction, some objective. . . . Everything that happens on the stage has a definite purpose.[1]

According to this principle, everything the actor does as the character should grow directly out of the needs of the character, so that the "inner" world of the character and the "outer" world of the performance are unified. This is what Stanislavski called a "truthful" performance.

This book is based on Stanislavski's idea. The central concept is that at each moment of the performance, your character wants something (your *need*), which makes you do something (your *action*) in an effort to achieve a desired goal (your *objective*). Some schools of acting use the terms *intention* or *task* instead of *objective,* but they all mean the same thing.

To put it even more simply, *need causes an action directed toward an objective.* We will explore each element of this central idea in later steps, but for now, reread it aloud several times, and feel the *flow* of energy from need to action toward objective.

The power of this approach is that your attention as an actor, in rehearsal and performance, is focused on the character's objective; this focus brings you many benefits, such as concentration, relaxation, economy, spontaneity, and reduction in self-awareness. Best of all, however, this focus helps to put you *into* your character in an active way: You *want* what the character wants in his or her circumstances, and you *do* what the character does to try to get it. This gives you a living experience of the character and leads to what Stanislavski called **transformation** as you become a new version of yourself by needing and doing what the character needs and does as if the needs and actions were your own (more on this in the next step).

---

[1]Constantin Stanislavski, *An Actor's Handbook,* trans. and ed. Elizabeth Reynolds Hapgood (New York: Theatre Arts Books, 1936), p. 8. Copyright © 1936, 1961, 1963 by Elizabeth Reynolds Hapgood.

PUBLIC SOLITUDE

Stanislavski tells of an acting student who, like many of us, suffered from stage fright. The student became tense and distracted on stage because he was overly aware of being watched. One day, his teacher gave him the simple task of counting the floorboards on the stage. The student soon became totally engrossed in this task. When he finished, he realized that it was the first time he had been on stage without self-consciousness. Surprisingly to him, the experience was liberating and exhilarating. Stanislavski points out that it was the student's total focus on his task that had allowed him to forget about being watched. He was *fully in action* and therefore became unself-conscious.

From this experience, Stanislavski developed his principle of the "dramatic task," or the *objective*.

Instead of counting floorboards, you can focus your full awareness on what your character is trying to achieve at any given moment. When you become so engrossed in this objective that your self-consciousness is greatly reduced, you have achieved the condition Stanislavski called **public solitude**. Public solitude is the ability to experience yourself as though you were in private, even though you are in public. We can see public solitude in real life: An athlete making a play in front of millions of spectators is aware only of the play and may "forget" the spectators entirely. You yourself at times have been so engrossed in what you were doing that you forgot you were in public.

People who are fully in action are automatically in public solitude. The actor who is totally focused on a character's objective can forget that an audience or a camera is watching. It is at such moments of public solitude that self-consciousness and fear are conquered. The objective serves the actor in the same way that a mantra serves a meditator, as a focus of attention that reduces self-awareness. It has been called "a bone thrown to the barking dog of the ego." Here is a simple exercise to help you begin to experience this focus of attention on an objective.

EXERCISE 6.1: A SIMPLE TASK

Select a simple physical activity that requires great concentration, such as building a house of cards, counting the floorboards or tiles on the floor, or balancing a stick on your nose. Perform this task in front of your class; can you allow yourself to become so absorbed in it that you "forget" that you are in front of an audience?

DUAL CONSCIOUSNESS

There is a danger in public solitude, however. Some young actors tend to focus so much on the solitude that they begin to ignore the requirements of being in public. They try to achieve some sort of trancelike state in which they lose artistic control and their sense of performance. But public solitude is not like a trance. Like the athlete, you should remain in control, fully aware of your task, and even though you have "forgotten" about the spectators or the camera, they should still be in the background of your awareness.

This, then, is the question: Can you be completely engrossed in the action and world of your character and simultaneously be aware of the demands of performance, making the artistic choices required to express your action in a public form worthy of your audience's or the camera's attention? This question is answered by your capacity for **dual consciousness**, your ability to function on more than one level of awareness at a time. As one of Stanislavski's students put it after a successful performance:

> I divided myself, as it were, into two personalities. One continued as [the character], the other was an observer [the actor]. Strangely enough this duality not only did not impede, it actually promoted my creative work. It encouraged and lent impetus to it.[2]

The two levels of consciousness, then, are that of the *character* pursuing his or her objective and that of the *actor* observing and adjusting the performance for the sake of the spectators or the camera.

Different performance situations may require more or less emphasis on one level of consciousness or the other. In television sketch comedy, for instance, we may allow a bit more of the actor awareness to be present in the performance; this explains why stand-up comedians are often successful in television sitcoms even though they may not be very skillful actors in the traditional sense. In naturalistic stage plays, however, we strive to reduce our actor consciousness to the minimum. For serious dramatic work for the camera, the actor must be completely invisible, leaving only the character behind. In fact, we say that the camera requires "no acting" at all. Even in this case, however, you do not lose your actor consciousness completely, nor do you want to. If you did, you would lose your ability to make artistic choices.

Dual consciousness may sound difficult, but it is really a very natural ability. When you were a child, a puddle easily became a vast ocean, but it didn't need to stop being a puddle. You hadn't learned yet that something isn't supposed to be two different things at once, and that we aren't supposed to be in two different realities at the same time. As an actor, you will have to forget your adult logic and allow yourself to rediscover this childhood ability to make believe, to joyfully enter the world of fantasy.

Many actors say that they chose acting as a career specifically because it gives them a chance to use their imaginations in the most complete way possible. Patrick Stewart, best known as Captain Picard on *Star Trek: The Next Generation* (and who is also a great Shakespearean actor), once told me, "What first attracted me to acting was the fantasy world of the theater into which I could escape from the much less pleasant world of my childhood." Another great actor, Sir Alec Guinness, spoke of acting as a way to escape from "my dreary old life."

---

[2]Constantin Stanislavski, *An Actor's Handbook,* trans. and ed. Elizabeth Reynolds Hapgood (New York: Theatre Arts Books, 1936), p. 9. Copyright © 1936, 1961, 1963 by Elizabeth Reynolds Hapgood.

EXERCISE 6.2: MAKING BELIEVE

Repeat the simple task exercise (6.1), but this time give yourself a character and a dramatic situation that raises the stakes. If your task was to build a house of cards, perhaps you could be a condemned man about to be executed, waiting for the governor to phone with your pardon. See if you can relax and accept the character's reality. Are you able to hold the dual awareness of your character's world and your actor's concerns?

INDICATING

Acting students commonly do too much on stage. They are afraid that it is not enough to simply do what their character is doing; they try to embellish, to show us how the character feels, or what kind of person the character is. They posture, exaggerate their emotions, use excessive gestures and facial expressions, and take on a false voice. Their performance is saying something like, "Hey, look at how angry I am," or "Look at what a villain I am."

This excessive behavior is called *indicating*. You are indicating when you are *showing* the audience something about the character instead of simply *doing* what the character does. Actors indicate for various reasons. Some feel unworthy of the audience's attention and think they have to work hard to earn it; some indicate because they are afraid of losing control over the performance; others simply think it "feels" the way they think acting should feel.

No matter the reason, indicating spoils the performance for the audience. It is part of the fun for the spectators to figure out for themselves how the character feels and what kind of person he or she is. Spectators do this by experiencing the actions of the character and discovering how they would feel if they did the same things in the same circumstances. Your job is to present the truthful evidence of the character's living action and leave the judgment and interpretation to the audience. If instead you *show* the audience how to feel about the character by indicating, you have created a performance *about* the character instead of presenting the character him- or herself. The audience may get the message but won't feel involved.

Since indicating is often the result of trying to do too much, economy of performance can help you to avoid it. Stanislavski often encouraged his actors to "cut eighty percent," to distill the performance to its essence. You must evaluate each element of the performance, retaining only that which contributes directly to a truthful expression of the character's action. As we often say, "Less is more," but of course it must be the correct "less."

Even after you have created a truthful moment, in rehearsal or performance, another form of indicating may befall you when you attempt to recreate that success in subsequent performances. Instead of having the courage to go back to the beginning and re-experience the entire process that produced the successful moment, you may be tempted to "play the result" and recreate the external form without reliving the internal process. This is a special danger in long runs of plays or in repeated takes in filming, when actors have to perform the same action over and over again. The essence of good acting, then, is to do what the character does, completely and precisely *as if for the first time and without adding anything superfluous.*

It is likely that you were guilty of some indicating when you were making believe in the previous exercise. You can learn to recognize indicating and avoid it by surrendering fully to your action. When you catch yourself *showing,* get back to *doing.* Repeat the previous exercise with this in mind.

EXERCISE 6.3: INDICATING

Repeat the Making Believe exercise (6.2), but this time ask your audience members to signal by making some sort of noise whenever they feel that you are indicating. Compare their feedback with your own sense of being in action. Did you know when you were indicating? How strong is your impulse to *show* instead of *do,* or to do too much?

RAISING THE STAKES

We began by saying that you "act" in everyday life when you do things in order to get what you want or need. The art of acting is based on this everyday process, but in performance, actions and their expression must be heightened and purified for artistic purposes. In the steps that follow, you will learn specific techniques to achieve this, but for now, let's consider the principles involved in making actions stageworthy.

Trying to do something really important in real life commands your whole attention, and all your energy and awareness flow through your action toward your objective. In acting, we say that a person fully committed to an important objective is **in action**. You have seen people with this kind of total commitment to an action: an athlete executing a difficult play, people arguing a deeply felt issue, a student studying for a big test, lovers wooing. All these people are in action because *they have an objective that is so personally significant that they are totally focused on what they are doing.* The more important the objective, the stronger the action and the more complete the focus. In acting, we call this **raising the stakes**.

There are various ways of raising the stakes. A good writer will often provide a scene with circumstances that raise the stakes by giving the outcome special significance, by creating some obstacle to the action, or by creating a deadline that encourages a sense of urgency. Actors learn to recognize these conditions and make the most of them in playing a scene.

You can also raise the stakes for yourself by finding in the character's situation some need or objective that has true personal significance for you. One way to do this is to make a **substitution** for the character's need with some analogous need or objective that touches you personally. If Willy Loman needs to get a sales assignment that won't require driving, for instance, perhaps that can remind you of your need to get a particular role in a play or to get admitted to a certain school. This kind of substitution will often happen automatically in rehearsal as you begin to experience the world and actions of the character and are reminded of similar needs, beliefs, and circumstances from your own life. These can become the bedrock on which you will build the character, and no amount of "acting" can substitute for the real personal energy these connections give you.

EXERCISE 6.4: RAISING THE STAKES

Think about a time when something happened to you that made you try to do something really important, when you were fully in action and the stakes were high. Relive this incident in your imagination, and then try to recreate it as a scene for your class; enlist the participation of others in the class if necessary. Remember that your aim is to recreate the experience itself; avoid "showing" or "telling" about it.

There are several benefits to the actor in raising the stakes by finding needs, objectives, and circumstances that are personally important. First, people reveal a great deal about themselves when they are fully committed to an important action, perhaps more than at any other time; as we say, "Actions speak louder than words." Second, when people are fully in action, they are pouring all their energy and awareness into what they are doing and have none left over for deception or self-consciousness; as a result, we judge them as *authentic* and *believable*. Finally, we find people who are fully in action *compelling* to watch; they seem so alive and energized that they command our full attention.

One word of caution, however: Strong personal connections, such as your memory of some significant event in your past (what Stanislavski called a **sense** or **emotion memory**, or **recall**), must be judged for their appropriateness to the demands of the scene and the character; your aim is to live fully in the place of the character, not to make the character fit yourself. Acting is not merely self-*expression*; it is self-*expansion*. Such strong references may also overwhelm you and cause you to lose artistic control. The American acting teacher Lee Strasberg counseled his students to use only such memories that were at least seven years in the past, thinking that this distance in time would make the memories more manageable, but Stanislavski warned that such memories may actually become more powerful over time. In any case, personal material is a potential source of great enrichment for the actor, but it must be used with care and discrimination.

To sum up: Being in action makes you more *alive, authentic, believable*, and *compelling*. In addition, being in action can help the actor to conquer those great enemies, self-consciousness and stage fright. These are all powerful reasons that being in action, being fully focused on a personally significant objective, is the best condition for you as an actor.

Summary of Step 6

Drama shows us something happening as if before our eyes and for the first time. Thus, the good actor's performance is not *about* the character; it *is* the character living before our eyes as if for the first time. For this reason, we say that acting is doing, not showing or telling. Stanislavski based his system on the idea that everything an actor does in a performance has to be justified by connecting it to an internal need in the character. The main idea is that need causes an action directed toward an objective.

When you are totally focused on your dramatic task, you lose self-consciousness and undue awareness of the audience. Stanislavski called this public solitude. However, you never lose total awareness of the performance; rather you are able to operate on two levels simultaneously, the level of the character and his or her needs and world and the level of the actor making artistic choices. This essential ability is called dual consciousness. Different kinds of performance require different emphases on these two levels of consciousness.

Beginning actors often do too much; instead of simply doing what the characters do, these actors think they need to show the audience how the characters feel or what kind of people the characters are. When you *show* instead of *do,* you are indicating, and you lose the economy of a truthful performance. The audience may understand but won't believe or feel involved.

In everyday life, people are in action when they have an objective that is so personally significant that they are totally focused on what they are doing; in acting, we call this raising the stakes. A good writer will often provide circumstances that raise the stakes. An actor can also raise the stakes for him- or herself by finding in the character's situation some need or objective that has true personal significance, as long as artistic purpose and control are maintained.

Being in action makes you more alive, authentic, believable, and compelling. In addition, being in action can help the actor to conquer those great enemies, self-consciousness and stage fright. Being in action, being fully focused on a personally significant objective, is the best condition for you as an actor.

7

Action, Emotion, and Character: The Magic If

Now it is time to put your sense of action to work within the context of a scene. We will begin with a simple improvisation. Keep this exercise simple; it doesn't need to be long, complicated, witty, or dramatic. Just let it be as real and natural as possible. Go with whatever comes up, and see where it leads.

EXERCISE 7.1: A SIMPLE ACTION SCENE

With a partner, select a simple situation in which one of you wants to do something (e.g., to leave the room) while the other has a contradictory objective (e.g., to make him or her stay). Think of a circumstance that raises the stakes: a deadline or consequence that creates urgency.

1. Without premeditation and with a minimum of words, both partners attempt to achieve their objectives in the most simple, direct terms.
2. Repeat the exercise, but this time each of you privately invents a powerful *need* for doing what you are doing. For example, one of you might imagine that if the other gets out, he or she will hurt someone you love; the other might imagine that he or she needs to get out to save a loved one. You needn't share or communicate what your needs are, nor do you and your partner need to agree on your needs.
3. Repeat the exercise again, this time imagining that you are both in a place where you cannot make much noise or movement, such as in a public library or at a funeral.

4. Discuss the experience of this exercise:

    a. Did you maintain your awareness of your objective throughout?

    b. Did you adjust what you did in reaction to what your partner did?

    c. What was the effect of adding strong needs?

    d. What was the effect of changing the circumstance?

    e. Did you notice how emotion and even a sense of character arose naturally from the action of the exercise?

ACTION AND EMOTION

In this exercise, you probably found that you began to experience emotion naturally, without trying, as you pursued your objective. People commonly think that one of an actor's main jobs is to portray strong emotions, and although emotion can be an important part of a performance, a good actor does not approach the work in this way. Genuine and specific emotion is achieved—on stage as in life—only as the *result* of trying to do something important, as in this exercise. This is how emotion works in real life; your emotions spring from your efforts to get what you want. Think of something you want desperately: If you get it, you are happy; if you don't, you are sad. If you don't get what you want and it is not your fault, you feel angry; when you don't get what you want and you don't know why, you feel afraid or frustrated. In all these cases, you acted on your need first, and emotion followed; so it should be in performance. *Action produces emotion, not the other way around.*

Likewise, in the acting process, actors too often think that they must *feel* something before they *do* anything. You sometimes hear them say, "I don't feel it yet." Of course you want to find the emotional state of your character so that your actions will have the proper quality and tone, but finding the right emotion is a *process,* and the emotion is the *result* of the process, not its starting point. You must *do* before you can *feel.* Even if a script gives you an indication of your character's emotional condition in a scene, you should not play that emotion; rather you will find it by experiencing the character's action while pursuing his or her objective in a way that results in the correct emotion. Trying to generate the emotion first is an unreliable and exhausting method that denies the way in which emotion functions in real life.

To sum up: You begin work not with the emotion but with the material you get from the script—the words your character says and the actions they convey—and as you experience the action, you discover the emotional life that it evokes. In other words, you *do* things in order to fulfill a need, and emotion naturally results from that doing. Trying to shortcut this process, to create an emotion for its own sake, is mere trickery lacking in truth for both actor and audience.

CHARACTER AND THE MAGIC IF

In the same way that emotion arises from action, character emerges from action as well. This is how it happens in real life, too, where we call character "personality."

Think about how your own personality has developed over the years and how often you "create a character" in real life. You play a role every time you enter a social situation. In various circumstances and relationships, you pursue your needs by behaving in certain ways, doing and saying certain things in certain ways to other people and reacting to the things they do and say to you. It is this interaction with your world, this give-and-take of acting and reacting, that shapes and expresses your character in everyday life. And it is an ongoing process: As your circumstances, needs, and relationships change, they cause changes in you as a person.

In fact, you play several roles every day—student, son or daughter, friend, employee; each has its own appropriate behavior, speech, thought, and feelings—your own little cast of characters! This fact was noticed many years ago by the psychologist William James, who said that our personalities are actually composed of many social roles. He called these roles our various *me's*. Behind the me's, of course, is one consciousness, which he called our *I*. But our I is not rigid and is expressed through all of our me's, even though some of them may be quite different from one another.

We may even experience situations in which two or more of our me's come into conflict with one another. If you are busy being "buddy" with your friends or "lover" with that special other, the arrival of a boss or parents may cause an uncomfortable conflict between your roles as buddy and employee or as lover and son or daughter. Such situations are inherently dramatic and often occur in plays, as when Hamlet is torn between the roles of son to Gertrude, lover to Ophelia, friend to Rosencrantz and Guildenstern, and avenger of his father.

EXERCISE 7.2: ROLE-PLAYING IN LIFE

Think about your own experience over the past few days. What roles did you play? How did your situations influence your behavior and feelings? Were there times when you had to switch roles rapidly or when your roles came into conflict?

As you think about how you play various roles in your life, you will also notice that your sense of "I" tends to flow into whichever "me" you are being at the moment. Some of your me's may be more—or less—comfortable than others, but they are all versions of you. If you are in a circumstance that forces you to behave in a certain way and you allow yourself to remain in that situation for a time, you start to become the person appropriate to that situation; you develop a new me, which in turn influences your I.

In the same way, when you perform as an actor on stage or screen, you will learn to let your I flow into the new me of each role you play, even when that me is quite different from your everyday self. The qualities of each new me have been determined by the writer, who has also created a new set of circumstances, a new world, in which the new me lives. One of your most important skills as an actor will be *to allow your I to flow fully and freely into the new me of the role and its world.* You do this not to "be yourself" but to develop a new *version* of yourself, perhaps one that is quite different from your everyday self but one that is nevertheless "natural" to you, truthful to the character and the character's world as created by the writer, and appropriate to the artistic purpose for which the role was created.

Stanislavski described this process as the **Magic If**. He urged the actor to ask, "*If* I were in the situation of the character, and *if* I wanted what the character wants, what would I do?" This approach can create interesting and useful improvisations, but it may also encourage actors to invent their own actions, which may not always be consistent with the specific demands of a given play. Although it is necessary for an actor to experience a character's needs, objectives, and actions as if they were his or her own, the actor does not have the freedom to alter the actions (the sayings and doings) specified by the script. Rather, the actor must *rediscover* the living process that lies beneath the dialogue and arrive at the result determined by the author.

We will therefore slightly modify Stanislavski's idea: *If* you allow yourself to live in the world of the character, and *if* you allow yourself to need what the character needs, and *if you allow yourself to do the things the character does* to try to satisfy those needs, you will naturally, "magically," start to modify your thoughts, feelings, behavior, and even your body and voice toward that new version of yourself that will be your special way of playing the role. This is true *transformation,* which is fundamental to our approach to the acting process and explains how character is created.

This ability to become a fictitious character, to completely believe in the Magic If and enter a make-believe world and character, is something we all had naturally as children. And it is this childlike capacity for make-believe that we need to rediscover as actors, however much we empower it through our adult sense of purpose and technique.

EXERCISE 7.3: CHARACTER IN LIFE

For the next few days, observe your own behavior toward those around you. Notice the ways you present yourself differently in various circumstances.

1. Notice changes in your physical behavior.
2. Notice changes in your voice, manner of speaking, and choice of words.
3. Notice your choice of clothing and the "props" you use.
4. Notice changes in the way you think and feel.
5. Most of all, notice how you naturally tend to "become" each of the roles you are playing.

As suggested earlier, consider keeping an actor's journal in which you record such experiences and observations as they occur. Such a journal can help to clarify your thinking and give form to your ongoing development.

THE ACTOR IN YOU

In Step 1, we said that when an actor creates a character, he or she uses a process that is similar to how personality is formed and evolves in everyday life. You are now able to understand this central concept more fully: In everyday life, we interact with our world and the people in it and the cumulative effect of those experiences and circumstances, especially those which are powerful or prolonged, shapes who we are; as our relationships or circumstances change, we change with them. It is this capacity for evolving as a person under the influence of new experiences that is the central mechanism of the acting process.

Rehearsals are an intensified and focused version of this real-life process through the operation of the Magic If; we imaginatively enter into the character's circumstances, experience his or her needs as if they were our own, form objectives aimed at satisfying those needs, and allow ourselves to do and say what the character does (his or her actions) to pursue those objectives. The power of these experiences shapes a new version of us, a new "me" for our "I," and so the dramatic character evolves in the same way that our personality evolves in real life. In Step 1, we quoted social psychologist Erving Goffman who said: ". . . life itself is a dramatically enacted thing. . . . In short, we all act better than we know how."[1]

We also noted, however, that these everyday abilities must be heightened, purified, and brought within the control of a purposeful discipline. We quoted acting teacher and psychologist Brian Bates: ". . . the actor must develop depths of self-knowledge and powers of expression far beyond those with which most of us are familiar."[2] You are now launched on the path of developing your everyday acting skills into the greater power of artistic technique. Up to this point, you have begun to prepare the physical, vocal, and mental skills you will need as an actor; you are now at a turning point. In the remaining steps, you will begin to apply yourself to the preparation of an actual scene, through which you will explore techniques and concepts that will help you to recognize, focus, and strengthen the natural actor you already are.

SELECTING YOUR SCENE

So far you have been introduced to the most fundamental concepts of the acting process. It is now time for you to begin to apply these concepts to an actual scene from a play. First, team up with a partner, and together choose a two-character scene that will serve you both well. Your scene may come from a stage play, film, or television script. Since you don't want to burden yourselves

---

[1]Erving Goffman, *The Presentation of Self in Everyday Life* (New York: Doubleday, 1959), pp. 71–74. Copyright © by Erving Goffman.
[2]Brian Bates, *The Way of the Actor* (Boston: Shambhala, 1987), p. 7.

with technical problems, such as handling difficult language or playing a far-different age, keep in mind the following qualities when selecting a scene:

1. A *realistic* and *contemporary* scene, written in language that is comfortable for you
2. Characters *close to you* in age and body type
3. A *short* scene that can be read aloud in no more than three to five minutes (or if necessary, a smaller section of a longer scene)
4. Most important, a scene that *touches* you personally in some way

There are many helpful anthologies of plays, films, TV scripts, and scenes for student actors. A list of useful plays and scene anthologies appears in Appendix B. Whatever the source of your scene, however, it is very important that you read the entire play or script from which the scene comes. Only in this way can you come to understand how your character, and the scene itself, functions within the story as a whole.

DRAMATIC FUNCTION REVISITED

Although the aim of Stanislavski's system is the creation of a truthful performance—that is, the actor is really doing what the character does and thereby has transformed him- or herself into a living embodiment of the character—Stanislavski was not satisfied unless the performance also correctly served the *needs of the play*. He stressed that an actor cannot use his or her transformational skill for its own sake, but rather strives to discover how every moment of the performance contributes to *the reason that the play was written*. This is the concept we spoke of in Step 1 as *dramatic function*.

In each play, every member of the cast must understand the meaning of the whole (the reason that the play was written) and how his or her character contributes to the whole (the character's dramatic function). There are two main ways that characters may serve a story: (a) by advancing the plot through their actions and (b) by contributing to the meaning of the play through the values that they and their actions express. In terms of the plot, your character may do things that drive the plot forward, may be a "foil" to frustrate the objectives of another character, or may simply provide some information essential to the story. In terms of the meaning of the story, your character may represent certain values or present a contrast to the values of other characters, may be the spokesperson for one of several conflicting points of view, or may be an embodiment of some quality or some aspect of the conflict within the main character.

For example, in Arthur Miller's *Death of a Salesman*, the actors playing Willy Loman's neighbor, Charley, and the ghost of Willy's brother, Ben, must understand that their characters were created to present alternative ways of living between which Willy must choose. Unlike Willy, Charley accepts who he is and lives happily; Ben, in contrast, represents the American Dream, making a fortune by daring and struggle. If Willy could learn to live like Charley instead of Ben, it would save Willy's life. The actors playing the roles of Charley and

Ben must create their performances with this in mind. (Arthur Miller even provides a scene in which Willy tries to talk to both of them at the same time and becomes hopelessly trapped between them.)

EXERCISE 7.4: DRAMATIC FUNCTION

After reading the entire play or script from which your scene comes, work with your partner to determine in a general way the dramatic function of your scene and each of your characters. Answer these questions:

1. If this scene were cut from the story, what essential event, information, or change in relationships would be lost?
2. If each of your characters were eliminated from the story, what would be missing from the plot?
3. How would the meaning of the play suffer if your character were cut? Is there some value or point of view expressed by your character? Does your character contribute to an understanding of other characters?
4. With your partner, read the scene aloud to the group. Discuss your understanding of the dramatic functions of your characters.

It is important to understand that the ideas you develop at this early stage are only working assumptions and will be apt to change as your work on the scene progresses. An understanding of a play and of the dramatic function of a character is often discovered gradually throughout the rehearsal process. These early assumptions give you only a direction in which to begin the exploration of the rehearsal process, and they provide some general sense of priority in judging the value and correctness of discoveries made in rehearsal. You will continue to search for a fuller understanding of dramatic function throughout your work on the role.

Summary of Step 7

As in everyday life, action produces emotion and character, not the other way around. This principle is fundamental to our approach to the acting process and explains how character is created. According to William James, our personalities are composed of many social roles he called our me's; behind the me's there is one consciousness, our I. As an actor you will learn to let your I flow into the new me of each role so that it becomes "natural" to you, truthful to the character, and appropriate to the artistic purpose for which the role was created.

Stanislavski called this process the Magic If. If you live in the world of the character, and if you need what the character needs, and if you do the things the character does to satisfy those needs, you will naturally start to modify your thoughts, feelings, behavior, and even your body and voice; a new me begins to form—that new version of yourself that will be your special way of playing the role.

What an actor does, then, is similar to what you do every day in real life. In this sense, you are already an actor, and you already have many of the skills you will need to perform. It is the development of these everyday acting skills into the greater power of artistic technique that is the aim of your study.

Although the aim of Stanislavski's approach is the creation of a truthful performance—that is, the actor is really doing what the character does and thereby has transformed him- or herself into a living embodiment of the character—Stanislavski was not satisfied unless the performance also correctly served the needs of the play by fulfilling the character's dramatic function.

8

Defining Objectives and Actions

Baseball batters rehearse their stance, grip, swing, and breathing. They study opposing pitchers. At the plate, they take note of the wind and the position of the fielders. As they begin to swing at a pitch, however, they cease to be aware of all these things and focus their total awareness on the ball. This single objective allows them to channel all their energy into their action, the swing. Having this single objective allows the batter to synthesize all his or her rehearsed and intuitive skills into a single complete action of mind and body that has tremendous power.

For you as an actor, the "ball" is your character's objective, what he or she is trying to accomplish at any given moment. Your focus on this single objective at the moment of action will overcome self-consciousness and give you power and control. Being focused on an objective propels you into action as you attempt to get what you want or need. In this step, you will learn how to define your character's objectives (what he or she wants) and actions (what he or she does to get them) in the most useful way. But first, here is an enjoyable game that will give you the experience of pursuing an objective.

EXERCISE 8.1: GUARD AND THIEF

In this game, you and your partner are both blindfolded, or you can simply keep your eyes closed. One of you is the "guard"; the other is a "thief." The thief has the objective of crossing the room and touching the far wall; the guard has the objective of stopping the thief by touching him or her. When the thief is touched by the guard, he or she "dies." At first, the guard is defensive, reacting to the thief, who tries various strategies to get past the guard; but when the teacher calls "Attack," the guard goes on the attack and seeks out the thief, who tries to elude capture.

Discuss this exercise. How did shifting into attack mode raise the stakes, heighten perception, and enhance the drama of the game? Did you experience the focus and liberation of pursuing an important objective?

DEFINING USEFUL OBJECTIVES

Experience has proven that objectives become more effective when they have three main qualities:

1. An objective needs to be *singular;* that is, you need to focus your energy on one thing rather than diffuse it by trying to do several things at once. Imagine a batter trying to hit two balls at the same time!
2. The most useful objective is in the *present*—something you want right now. Although your character's needs may be rooted in the past and may be a step toward some larger, overall objective in the future, his or her action at this moment is directed toward an objective in the immediate present.
3. An objective must be *personally important* to you. As you have already learned, personalizing an objective will energize you and empower your action.

It is easy to remember these three requirements by the acronym SIP: *singular, immediate,* and *personal.*

A useful example comes from a scene in *Death of a Salesman* in which Willy, a traveling salesman who is having trouble driving, goes to see his boss, Howard. Willy has an overall *scene objective* of wanting to persuade Howard to give him an assignment in town so he won't have to drive so much, but Willy has to pursue this scene objective one step at a time, through a series of *immediate objectives.* When he enters the scene, he sees Howard playing with a new recorder, so Willy's *immediate objective* is to get Howard to stop playing with the recorder and to pay attention.

This objective is *singular* and *immediate.* It is also supremely important in a *personal* way to Willy: If he can't get Howard's attention, he won't be able to ask for a job in town; if he doesn't get a job in town, he won't be able to be a successful salesman; if he can't be a successful salesman, he will think of himself as a failure in life. In this way, Willy's deepest, lifelong need for self-esteem lives in the present moment, and getting Howard's attention has all the urgency of a life-and-death struggle.

From this example, you can see that objectives work on three levels: *immediate* objectives are steps toward a *scene* objective, and the scene objective is a step toward a character's life goal, which we call his or her **superobjective** (more about this in Step 14). Your character will have one immediate objective within each **beat** of a scene; when characters in a scene change their objectives or the strategy they are using to achieve their objectives, each change creates a new *beat* (unit of action). A **beat change** can be felt as a change in the flow of the action, because the action of the scene "turns a corner" and moves in a new direction at that point. (We will explore this in greater detail later in this step.)

PLAYABLE STRATEGIC ACTIONS

Since your energy must continually flow outward into the scene in order to keep the story moving, you want to define your actions in the most **playable** (i.e., *active*) way possible. First, you use a *simple **verb** phrase in transitive form*—that is, a verb that *involves* a *doing* directed *toward* someone else, such as "to flatter him." You avoid forms of the verb *to be* because this verb has no external object and its energy turns back on its subject, the *doer*. You are never interested, for example, in "being angry" or "being a victim"; these states of being are not playable because their energy is directed inward. Strive instead for a *doing* in which your energy flows toward an external object.

Next, you select a verb that carries a sense of the particular **strategy** chosen by your character to achieve the objective. As in real life, your character will naturally select an action that seems to offer the greatest chance for success in the given circumstances and in relation to the other person(s) in the scene.

Let's return to the Willy Loman scene and see how you might describe your action if you were playing Willy. You have just entered; you desperately need to get a job in town; you see Howard playing with the recorder. At this moment, you have the SIP objective of getting Howard to pay attention, but you want to do it in a way that will make him feel positive toward you. As a salesman, you instinctively appeal to something a "client" would be interested in, so you flatter Howard by praising the recorder and the stupid recording he has made of his family. The most complete description of your action and objective at this moment is *to flatter Howard by praising the recorder* (strategic action) in order *to get him to pay attention to me in a positive way* (objective).

While you are learning to act, it may help you to form such a complete verbal description of your objectives and actions. Remember, however, that these verbal descriptions are valuable only insofar as they contribute to your actual experience of playing the scene. The ability to describe something comes from the analytical left side of the brain, whereas the creative work of performance originates in the intuitive right side of the brain. Although they can complement and augment one another wonderfully, the two sometimes get in each other's way.

EXERCISE 8.2: DEFINING OBJECTIVES AND ACTIONS

Working with your partner, read through your scene aloud several times. Then go through the scene together, and define each of your objectives and actions.

1. Make each objective SIP.
2. Describe each action with a transitive verb phrase that expresses the strategy being used.

SUBTEXT

As do people in everyday life, a character will select an action that seems to offer the best chance for success in the given circumstances. Most often, this will be a direct action such as persuading, demanding, cajoling, or begging. However, sometimes there is an obstacle to direct action, which may be *internal,* like Willy's fear of angering Howard because he knows that Howard would not be eager to give him a spot in town, or *external,* like Howard's obsession with the recorder. At such times, the character will try, as people do in everyday life, to get around the obstacle through an indirect approach, by saying or doing one thing when they really mean or want something else. In this case, although Willy *seems* to be enjoying Howard's recording, he actually wants to get Howard to turn it off and pay attention. This kind of "hidden agenda" is called a **subtext**, because there is a difference between the surface activity, the text, and the hidden objective, the subtext. (Howard has his own subtext; he may be using the recorder to avoid a confrontation with Willy.)

Some approaches to acting use the term *subtext* not only to describe indirect action, but to refer to *all* the inner motivations that drive a character's external actions. In the *Death of a Salesman* scene, for example, Willy's subtext is "to get a spot in town so I don't have to drive anymore," and Howard's subtext may be "to finally fire Willy." From this point of view, there is *always* a subtext, that inner source of need that Stanislavski called the "spiritual" action that drives the external "physical" action. By connecting the two, we *justify* the external action.

How do you play a subtext? *You don't!* You will find that a good writer always provides a surface activity through which the subtext may be expressed— in this case, Willy's pretended interest in the recorder. You must accept this surface activity as your immediate action: Do not attempt to bring the subtext to the surface by indicating it, by performing in a way that says, "I'm only pretending to be interested; what I really want is his attention." Doing so will destroy the reality of the scene. For one thing, if the audience members can see Willy's subtext, they will wonder why Howard can't. Trust that your simple awareness of the subtext will be enough to properly color your actions. In fact, subtext will often work even if you are unaware of it, since those in the audience can see the disparity between your behavior and their understanding of the real needs of the character. Trust the audience to deduce the subtext from the situation. It is part of the fun for audience members to figure this out for themselves; if you make it obvious, they may understand, but they won't feel involved.

EXERCISE 8.3: SUBTEXT

1. Again, read through your scene aloud with your partner. Begin to feel the objectives you have identified propelling you and the scene itself forward. Then together, examine the objectives you defined in the previous exercise, and see if any of them involve an *indirect* strategy.

    a. If so, why can't the action be expressed directly? What is the obstacle?

    b. Is the obstacle, if any, internal or external?

    c. Does your character therefore have a subtext or hidden agenda?

2. Whether there is indirect action or not, try to feel the underlying needs and objectives driving your character's action. Can you experience the subtext without bringing it to the surface of the scene?

NOT DOING

There is always at least one alternative available to a character in any situation, and that is the choice to *not* act—to suppress or delay action. Although we often think of such "not doing" as passivity, it can actually be a strong form of action; in fact, it takes more effort to hold a strong impulse in than it does to let it out. This can be very useful in drama: When a character chooses to suppress an impulse, that unresolved energy is reflected back into that character and builds up to become a source of increasing dynamic tension. You know from your own experience that the longer an important need is suppressed, the stronger it becomes. This fact helps writers to build suspense in a play or film. Shakespeare's Hamlet, for example, spends a great deal of time wondering whether to avenge his father's murder; he finds one excuse after another for not acting on his need. There is a wonderful scene in the middle of the play, for instance, in which Hamlet decides *not* to kill Claudius despite a perfect opportunity to do so. We begin to wonder, How much longer will he wait? What will happen? The tension becomes greater and greater with each passing scene. In the last scene of the play, circumstance does not permit him to delay any longer, and his action finally explodes.

    In everyday life we call this choice to "not do" **suppression**, which literally means "pushing down." Viewed in this way, there are no passive characters on the stage or screen; there are only characters who are aroused but then choose *not* to act. Unlike a novelist, who can take us inside a character's mind, a playwright can imply suppressed actions only within the context of a scene, so you will have to use your imagination to discover them. Examine your scene moment by moment, and ask yourself, Is there anything my character wants to do here but doesn't?

    The choice to not act is a strong and playable action. To play a "not doing," simply identify what the character wants to do but doesn't. Let yourself feel strongly the need to act and also the effort required to suppress the action. This process turns the "not doing" into a "doing" and makes it playable and dramatic.

EXERCISE 8.4: SUPPRESSION

Work through your scene with your partner. Look for any suppressed actions. Discuss any you find. Then read through your scene with this awareness: Avoid indicating the suppressed actions, but allow yourself to experience them fully.

OBSTACLES AND COUNTERACTIONS

Since plays, films, and TV shows are about people interacting dramatically with one another, you must understand your character's objectives in ways that not only energize and focus you by being SIP and transitive, but also connect you with the other characters in the scene. The best way to achieve connectedness is to think of your objective as being *in* the other character, something specific you need from that person. The best objective, then, is *a change you want to bring about in the other character.*

In life, when we do something to try to make a change in someone else, we watch to see if what we are doing is working; if it is not, we try something else. This should be true on stage as well. Ask yourself, How will I know I am achieving my objective? What changes might I see in the other character that will indicate that my approach is working?

This sort of observable change that you want to bring about in the other character is the best way to define your objective. One acting teacher even encouraged his actors to think of their objective as "a change in the other character's eyes." In the Willy Loman scene, for instance, your first objective might be *to get Howard to look at me with interest.* Your full attention is on him, watching to see if your behavior is indeed producing the desired effect, or whether you might have to try a different approach (which in this case you eventually do).

Notice how each of your objectives affects the other character and vice versa. You are each evoking a reaction in the other, and you may also be presenting *obstacles* to one another's actions. In the most extreme cases, your objectives may be in direct contradiction, and you may be acting *counter* to one another. Howard's insistence that Willy listen to the recording of his family, for example, is a *counteraction* to Willy's attempts to get Howard's attention. It is likely, in fact, that Howard is deliberately using the recording to avoid Willy. Such obstacles and counteractions are important to the development of the drama of a scene, and by playing *into* one another you get full value from them.

EXERCISE 8.5: CONNECTING THE ACTION

1. Go through your scene, and define each of your objectives as a change in the other character.
2. Identify how your characters provide obstacles and counteractions to one another so as to heighten the drama.
3. Rehearse the scene with this awareness. Carry your scripts, but begin to move; don't worry about blocking, but simply begin to allow your action to express itself in bodily movement within the space of the playing area.
4. Discuss the scene with your partner or class. Did you achieve a stronger interaction? Did the action of the scene flow better?

Summary of Step 8

The best focus for an actor's awareness is the character's objective (what he or she wants), from which flows the character's action (what he or she does to try to get it). This focus on a single objective at the moment of action will overcome self-consciousness and give you power and control.

Objectives become more effective when they are SIP: singular, immediate, and personal. Actions are best defined actively, using a simple verb phrase in transitive form. Avoid forms of the verb "to be" because their energy turns back upon the subject. Your verb should reflect the particular strategy chosen by your character to achieve the objective.

When there is an internal or external obstacle that prevents direct action, characters may try to get around the obstacle through an indirect approach; this kind of hidden agenda is a subtext. Never try to bring a subtext to the surface! A character may also choose to *not* act, to suppress action, which helps to build suspense.

It is best to think of an objective as a change you want to bring about in the other character. Drama is heightened when characters present obstacles and counteractions to one another.

9

The Flow and Shape of Drama

In the previous step, we stressed that you must understand your objectives and actions in a way that causes you to interact with the other characters to produce a flow of dramatic action that builds suspense and provides a satisfying dramatic experience. This flow is created when something happens to you—you hear something or see something—that arouses you in some way, and you then say or do something in reaction. In turn, your action—your saying or doing—causes a reaction in some other character, and so on. Thus, the energy of the scene flows, being traded between you and the other characters as you *act and react* to one another. Here is an exercise to help you experience that flow.

EXERCISE 9.1: IMPULSE CIRCLE

1. With your entire group, sit about eighteen inches apart in a large circle, in chairs or on the floor. Make the circle perfectly round. All group members put their left hands out palm up, and then rest their right hands lightly on top of the left hands of those to their right. The leader starts with a small, clean slap with his or her right hand. The slap is then passed on from person to person around the circle. Once the slap is moving well, try the following experiments:

   a. Focus your awareness on the slap as it moves around the circle. Begin to experience it as having a life of its own. Notice how it changes when you all do this.

   b. Now allow the slap to move as quickly as it can. See what happens when you "get out of its way." Do not

force it to go faster; simply relax and react to it as instantaneously as possible.

    c. Now let the slap slow down. See how slow it can go without
dying. Keep the external slap sharp and quick, but slow
down the inner impulse as it travels within each of you.
Become aware of how the slap flows through both internal
and external phases.

2. Drop your hands and discuss the many ways in which this exercise is like a scene in a performance. Consider these questions:

    a. What made it possible for the slap to flow around the
group? How is this similar to the way a scene should flow in
a performance?

    b. As you experienced the slap as having a life of its own, how
did the nature of the flow change? Did your own experience
of it change?

    c. Did allowing it to be the focus of your awareness reduce
your self-consciousness?

    d. How much of the time was the slap "invisible" as a purely
internal action? When the slap was slow, were there times
when it was completely internal? Were such moments any
less dramatic?

    e. What was different about the experience when the slap was
moving slowly? What did you need to do to support its life,
even while it was passing through the others in the circle?

    f. What are some of the ways in which a scene can "die"?
What are some of the ways in which we can fail to "pass it
on"? How do actors make similar mistakes in performance?

3. Repeat the exercise using a sound such as "ho" instead of
a slap.

Repeat this exercise on subsequent days for a good group
warm-up.

INTERNAL AND EXTERNAL ACTION

In this exercise you experienced how energy passes between people, taking
both external and internal forms. It is external when someone is saying or
doing something, but much of the time it is internal as each participant receives
the energy from others, reacts to it internally, and then passes it on through
external action. In the same way, a scene in a play or screenplay depends on
energy flowing from character to character as each one *reacts* internally and
then *acts* externally toward the other.

    When energy is passed from one character to another, we call it an
interaction (some acting teachers call it a **moment**). Each interaction is a connection in the flow of action and reaction that moves the scene and the entire
story. Actors work hard to build each interaction in a scene, to make each of

them real, and to make sure each moves toward the ultimate destination of the scene and the story as a whole.

It is important to understand that action is not just external activity. A cat watching a mouse hole is not moving at all, yet we recognize the drama in it. This is because action is felt even before it has shown itself in external activity; it lives even in the *potential* for doing. At such moments, the **inner action** is living inside us, waiting to erupt into the outside world. Stanislavski called inner action **spiritual action** and the outer action it produces *physical action*:

> The creation of the physical life is half the work on a role because, like us, a role has two natures, physical and spiritual. . . . a role on the stage, more than action in real life, must bring together the two lives—of external and internal action—in mutual effort to achieve a given purpose.[1]

When we have connected an external action with the internal action that motivates it, Stanislavski would say that we have **justified** the action. For Stanislavski it was this justification, this complete integration of internal and external action, that produced a truthful stage performance. Accordingly, his acting system was designed to bring about this integration. In the beginning, he used psychological techniques that were designed to work from the internal to the external (from the inside out). Later in the development of his method, he began to work from the external toward the internal (from the outside in). As he said, our inner condition is affected by our outer action just as much as our outer action is caused by our inner condition:

> The spirit cannot but respond to the actions of the body, provided of course that these are genuine, have a purpose.... [In this way] a part acquires inner content [through the development of outer actions.][2]

Many have wondered whether the actor should work from the inside out or from the outside in. Throughout the modern period, various techniques have been developed that fall on one side of this question or the other. In general, during the first half of the twentieth century the British acting tradition stressed the importance of externals in the acting process, working from the outside in, whereas the American tradition stressed the importance of internals, working from the inside out, most notably in the work of Lee Strasberg, founder of the Actors Studio, who placed great emphasis on Stanislavski's early psychological techniques called *emotion memory* and sense memory (more on these in later steps).

---

[1]Constantin Stanislavski, *Building a Character*, trans. Elizabeth Reynolds Hapgood (New York: Theatre Arts Books, 1949), pp. 218–236. Theatre Arts Books, 153 Waverly Place, New York, NY 10014.
[2]Constantin Stanislavski, *Creating a Role*, trans. Elizabeth Reynolds Hapgood (New York: Theatre Arts Books, 1961), p. 62.

Since the 1950s, however, most training programs on both sides of the Atlantic have tried to integrate these approaches. The aim is now for a total integration of internals and externals, because both are essential, as Stanislavski himself pointed out:

> External action acquires inner meaning and warmth from inner action, while [inner action] finds its expression only in physical terms.[3]

If your action consists only of external movement and speech unconnected to an inner energy, it will seem hollow and lifeless. But if your action lives only as inner intensity, without skillful outer expression, it will seem vague and self-indulgent. The most useful approach, then, is to avoid thinking of inner and outer action as being in any way separate. Imagine instead *a single flow of action that has both an inner phase and an outer phase.*

THE SHAPE OF DRAMA

The flow of action in the Impulse Circle exercise (9.1) was not necessarily dramatic. If a scene or play were to flow in this steady way, it would soon become boring. When Aristotle described the way a good drama works, he said that the best kind of play is driven by an underlying conflict that is developed as the characters interact with one another, producing a flow of dramatic action that rises as *suspense* builds, until it reaches a **crisis**, at which point it reverses and falls toward a **climax** and resolution. Aristotle used the terms *raveling* for the rising action and u*nraveling* for the falling action: The French word for "unraveling" is ***dénouement***, and this is the term we commonly use in theater for the resolution at the end of the play. This shape—a rising action building toward a turning point followed by a resolution—is something that writers work hard to build into a play and into each scene within the play. An actor must be able to recognize it and work to fulfill it, since it forms the fundamental rhythm of the performance. You can experience this shape through a simple exercise.

EXERCISE 9.2: A DRAMATIC BREATH

1. Take a single, complete breath that is as *dramatic* as you can make it. Don't think about it; just do it!
2. Now consider the things you did to make the breath more dramatic. If you are in a group situation, discuss this and see if there was something that everyone did.

When trying this exercise for the first time, most people exaggerate their breath, making it louder, they may also add movement to the breath to make it more visible. Some people take a faster or slower breath than normal. These

---

[3]Constantin Stanislavski, *An Actor's Handbook*, trans. and ed. Elizabeth Reynolds Hapgood (New York: Theatre Arts Books, 1936), p. 9. Copyright © 1936, 1961, 1963 by Elizabeth Reynolds Hapgood.

things, however, are limited to the external aspects of the breath; they serve to make the breath more *theatrical,* not necessarily more dramatic. Do you understand the difference? A sense of drama is deeper than such external considerations; it implies an experience that involves us in a more fundamental way and can take many different external forms.

Consider for a moment those situations in real life that are naturally dramatic. Let's use a sporting event as an example: What are the things that make for a really dramatic football, baseball, or basketball game? For one thing, games between teams that are evenly matched, especially when they are longtime rivals, can be special fun because the sense of **conflict** is greater. *Conflict* literally means "to strike together," so any situation in which two strong forces are opposed creates a sense of drama. Most plays and film scripts are driven by a central conflict between two opposing forces, usually embodied by a protagonist and an antagonist (in popular parlance, a hero and a villain.) But conflict can exist even within a single person: The most famous example is Hamlet, who is torn between his need to avenge the murder of his father and Hamlet's own moral intelligence, what one critic called a conflict between *will* and *reason.* Another example, in Tennessee Williams's *The Glass Menagerie,* is the central conflict within Tom, a conflict between independence and responsibility. Tom needs to leave home to find his own identity, but he feels an obligation to stay to help his sister and mother. This conflict is *universal* because all children feel something like it when it is time for them to leave the nest, even if their siblings and parents are not as needy as Laura and Amanda.

Besides having a strong conflict, a game can be more dramatic if it is more important or *significant.* Perhaps the championship is at stake, or the teams are long-standing rivals. These stakes are raised, and the higher the stakes, the greater the drama can be. In the dramatic breath exercise, some of you may have increased the importance of your breath by taking a deeper breath; this deeper breath contained more energy and was therefore more significant than normal. Notice, however, that a significant breath may not necessarily be bigger or louder; the significance of the breath depends not on these external qualities but on its inner *dynamic,* the amount of energy it contains. For example, imagine a situation in which you are hiding from a killer in a dark, silent room; your life depends on making no noise or movement. How would you breathe? Can you feel that your breathing is highly significant and dramatic even though it is invisible and inaudible? Similarly, the conflict underlying *The Glass Menagerie* is crucial to Tom's sense of himself; it is, in a psychological sense, a matter of life and death, but it is expressed through small actions, like going to the movies as an escape.

In addition to a strong conflict and high significance, the drama of a game depends on the *outcome being in doubt.* The closer the score of the game, the greater the drama can be; if one team gets too far ahead, we lose interest. Think back to your dramatic breath: How might you put the outcome of your breath in doubt? The best way would be to hold it; while you are holding it, others might wonder, When will he or she breathe out? This is suspense in its purest form: *an aroused energy that wants to be released but is literally "held up."* According to playwright David Mamet, the most important question in the theater is, What will happen?

If the suspense of a game can last to the very last play, the drama is tremendous. In the same way, the longer you hold your breath, the more the suspense *builds* toward a climax. This is a common strategy in plays; the outcome is held in doubt as long as possible, thereby raising the level of suspense higher and higher. We call this rise and fall of energy the **arc** of the play or scene, and the greater the arc, the greater the drama. In the exercise, you may have increased the arc of your breath by building to a high point and then releasing it more deeply. We enjoy this sense of release, which in drama is called the *climax.*

To sum up, then, our definition of a dramatic event is *a conflict of powerful forces in which the stakes are high and the outcome is in doubt, building to a crisis, which is followed by a climax.*

CRISIS

In a well-constructed play, the sequence of events (the **plot**) moves forward as suspense builds. This sequence begins when something happens (or is reported to have just happened) that establishes the underlying conflict of the play. This is called the *inciting incident.* There follows a series of *episodes* (each of them usually a **scene**) in which the conflict develops. During this period of rising energy and growing suspense, we begin to wonder, How will this come out? When the conflict is just on the verge of being resolved, suspense is at its peak. This moment of greatest suspense, as the outcome hangs in the balance, is called the *crisis* (the turning point). The function of everything that happens before the crisis is to lead toward it with *rising* energy, while everything after the crisis flows naturally from it with a *falling* sense of resolution.

Recall the single breath you took in Exercise 9.2. As you inhaled, the dynamic energy rose; when you began to hold the breath, the period of crisis began. The longer you held the breath, the more the suspense built; the exact moment when you decided to exhale ended the crisis, and the exhaling itself was the climax of the breath. This is the way most plays are shaped. The best way to identify the crisis of a play is to work backward from the end, looking for the moment at which the outcome of the play hangs most in the balance, the moment when the outcome is determined. Ask yourself: Given the way the story comes out, what is the last moment at which it might have turned out differently? (This strategy of "reading backward" is a valuable tool that you will also use in analyzing scenes in the next step.)

For example, in *The Glass Menagerie,* the idea of finding a gentleman caller who could marry Laura and thereby release Tom from his family obligations is established early, in the second scene of the play—this is the inciting incident. The main body of the play works out the details of the plan, and suspense mounts as Tom actually manages to bring Jim home. Suspense peaks as Jim dances with Laura and we sense that perhaps the plan might actually succeed;

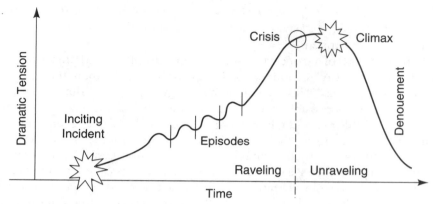

FIGURE 9.1 The Shape of Drama.

if it does, Jim will take over as the man of the house, and Tom will be released from his obligation without guilt. Sadly, however, the crisis reveals that the plan cannot work as Jim tells Laura that he is in love with someone else:

LAURA *[FAINTLY]*:   You—won't—call again?

JIM: No, Laura, I can't.

The climax flows quickly from this; Laura falls back even more deeply into her dependency, Amanda blames Tom for the failure of the plan, and Tom finally storms out for good, wracked by guilt.

This, then, is the fundamental shape of Western drama: an inciting incident establishes a fundamental conflict, followed by episodes (scenes) of rising conflict and suspense that lead up to a crisis, which is followed by a climax and resolution (see Figure 9.1). It is a shape common to all of the performing arts—symphonies and ballets have it, too. It is the fundamental unit of rhythm, because it is the shape of a muscular contraction and relaxation. It is the fundamental shape of life itself, from birth to death, and it lives even within a single breath.

EXERCISE 9.3: THE SHAPE OF YOUR PLAY

Working with your scene partner, discuss your play. Think backward from the end:

1. What is the basic conflict?
2. What makes this conflict significant? What is at stake?
3. What is the source of suspense? How is the outcome kept in doubt?
4. Where is the crisis, when the conflict is on the verge of being resolved? Is the crisis prolonged over a period time?
5. What is the climax that follows?

Summary of Step 9

A scene lives because of the energy flowing from character to character as they interact through the flow of action and reaction, which moves the scene forward and eventually creates the unfolding of the entire story. Action has both an internal and an external form. If action consists only of external activity unconnected to an inner energy, it seems hollow and lifeless; if it is only an inner intensity, without skillful outer expression, it seems vague and self-indulgent. Stanislavski believed it was the complete integration of internal and external action, which he called justification, that produced a truthful stage performance. The most useful approach is to think of a single flow of action that has both an inner phase and an outer phase.

A dramatic event begins with a conflict in which the stakes are high and the outcome is in doubt and builds toward a climax. In a well-structured play, an inciting incident establishes a fundamental conflict, followed by episodes of rising conflict and suspense, which lead to a crisis that is followed by a resolution in the climax.

10

Exploring Scene Structure and the Given Circumstances

Rehearsing a scene is much like making a map of an unknown territory. You and your partner, through trial and error, discover for yourselves the pathway of the scene's energy, the logic of the flow of cause and effect hidden beneath the surface of the dialogue. You can best begin by understanding the dramatic purpose of the scene within the story as a whole: Ask yourselves, What happens in this scene that changes the world of the play? Why couldn't this scene be cut from the story? Understanding the scene's purpose can help to guide your rehearsal exploration and establish priorities that will make your work more efficient.

Next, you begin to explore the pathway through which the scene's energy flows, interaction by interaction, and the shape that the writer has given to this flow. Your work so far has helped you to understand that the energy of the scene will flow up toward the *scene crisis* and then away from it. The crisis of the scene is the major milestone on the journey you and your partner are discovering. It may be obvious in your initial analysis of the scene, or it may take some experimenting in rehearsal to find it, but your exploration will be more efficient if you agree on it in a general way as you set out.

The analysis of a scene's crisis is approached in the same way as the overall play; you work backward from the end of the scene, looking for the moment in which the outcome of the scene hangs most in the balance, the moment when the outcome of the scene is determined. Ask yourself: Given the way the scene comes out, what is the last moment at which it might have turned out differently? For example, consider again the scene in *Death of a Salesman* in which Willy goes to see his boss, Howard, to persuade him to give him an assignment in town; that is Willy's scene objective. After Willy has made his request and tried several different strategies to win his objective, the crisis occurs when Howard not only refuses his request, but fires him as well. The moment before Howard decides to tell Willy he is being fired is the moment of crisis, the turning point, of the scene.

You will notice that moments of crisis are almost always choices made by one of the characters, and they usually occur "between the lines." You will also notice that unlike entire plays, scenes do not usually have a strong sense of resolution or climax after the crisis, since they must move the story forward into the next scene.

Although you may analyze a scene's structure by breaking it down intellectually in this way at first, experienced actors usually approach structure intuitively, developing a shared rhythmic sense of the rise and fall of the scene's energy as they explore it in rehearsal. However you find it, your understanding of scene structure must finally live as a sort of underlying "dance" as you and your partner feel the energy of the scene moving and building toward the crisis and then flowing naturally from it.

EXERCISE 10.1: THE CRISIS OF YOUR SCENE

Working with your partner, answer these questions about your scene:

1. What is the major change in the world of the play that occurs in this scene? How does this scene cause the plot to progress? How does it enhance the meaning of the play?
2. What is the crisis of the scene, the moment when the outcome is determined?
3. How does this scene grow out of the scene before it and lead into the scene to follow?

Now read through the scene aloud; move around, holding your script. Don't worry about blocking; simply let your body move as you feel the changing rhythm of the scene. Feel how the action of the scene flows up toward the crisis and then flows from it.

UNITS OF ACTION, OR BEATS

Plays are usually divided into acts, acts into scenes, and scenes themselves may be divided into smaller units of action called **beats**. The word *beat* may come from *bit*, meaning "a small part." Stanislavski used the term "unit of action" for what we commonly call a beat today. In any case, a beat is the *smallest unit of dramatic action that has its own dramatic shape, with an underlying conflict and a rising action leading to a crisis.* Beats, like scenes, do not have much resolution, however, since they must lead us on into the next beat in order to continue the flow of the action within the scene.

For example, consider the beginning of the scene in *Death of a Salesman* when Willy enters and sees Howard playing with a new recorder. As we have said, Willy's scene objective is to get an assignment in town, but he must pursue this objective through a series of steps. When he sees Howard with the recorder, Willy's immediate objective is to get Howard to stop playing with the recorder and to pay attention to him. Ever the good salesman, Willy tries to flatter Howard and feign interest in the recorder. Soon he gets Howard's attention, when Howard looks up and says, "Say, aren't you supposed to be in Boston?" This is the turning point that ends the first beat of the scene; it is called a **beat change**.

This first beat of the scene has its own underlying conflict (Willy trying to get Howard's attention, Howard trying to ignore Willy) and a crisis (Howard finally giving up and paying attention to Willy). This beat is comprised of several interactions between Willy and Howard, but it is unified by the fact that each character has one immediate objective throughout (Willy to get attention, Howard to ignore Willy). When one of the characters changes his objective, the change leads us into a new beat (why isn't Willy in Boston?). This beat change can be felt as a change in the flow of the action of the scene as it turns a corner and moves in a new direction. Because this turn is felt as a pulse in the rhythm of the scene, the term *beat* is a good description of the musical shape of the flow of a scene's rhythm.

Your attention as an actor is on the immediate moment, the here and now, but you are also aware of how this moment contributes to the beat of which it is a part, how each beat contributes to the scene of which it is a part, and ultimately how each scene contributes to the overall structure of the play as a whole. Thus, every small unit of action is part of a larger pattern and derives its meaning and function from the way it fits into and contributes to that larger pattern. Again, the individual interactions between characters work together to form the units of action we call beats; the beats work together to form a scene; and the scenes flow together to lead us to the main crisis and climax of the entire story. This idea may be more easily understood by the muscles than the mind, so let's try a physical exercise to experience it.

EXERCISE 10.2: UNITS OF ACTION

Perform each of the following actions, and experience the dramatic potential of each. Remember to focus on the crisis in each pattern: Treat all that goes before as leading up to the crisis and all that follows as flowing from it.

1. Experience the dramatic shape of a single step. Find the crisis of one step, and tie your breathing to the shape of each step.
2. Experiment with differently shaped steps: a long rise, a long crisis, and a quick release; then a short rise, a short crisis, and a long release; and so on.
3. Take three steps experienced as one phrase, with the crisis in the third step. The first two steps have minicrises of their own, but they also lead up to the main crisis of the unit in the third step. Let your breath parallel the pattern of your steps.
4. Now try nine steps, divided into three units of three steps each, with the crisis of this larger pattern in the last group (as in Figure 10.1). Try it again with the crisis in the first group of steps.
5. Invent patterns of your own; add sound.

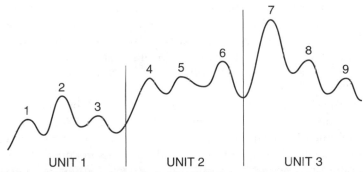

FIGURE 10.1   Units of Action. 9 steps divided into three units go together to produce one large pattern.

In this exercise you experienced small units of action forming a larger pattern of action that has a dramatic shape of its own. Likewise, these larger phrases can be connected into still larger patterns, which again have shapes of their own. On all these levels, the fundamental shape of rise, crisis, and release is the same, even though the proportion of the parts may be different.

This, then, is how the parts of a play or screenplay go together to make the whole: The smallest units of action, the individual *interactions* between characters, work together to form the units of action we call *beats,* each of which has a crisis of its own, which leads into the following beat. The beats work together to form a *scene,* which has a crisis of its own, and the scenes flow together to lead us to the *main crisis* of the entire story.

Let's take an example from a scene in *A Raisin in the Sun.* We begin with the given circumstances: It is morning on a work day in the tiny, crowded kitchen of the Lee apartment; as usual, Ruth is fixing breakfast for her husband, Walter. The night before, Walter's friend Willy suggested a scheme to open a liquor store. Willy's idea was that Walter, Willy, and another friend (Bobo) would each invest $10,000 to open the store. It was no coincidence that Walter's father had recently died, leaving a $10,000 life insurance payment; Willy knew this and concocted the whole scheme (as we will learn later) in order to cheat Walter out of his money. But for now, Walter thinks the scheme is legitimate, and he comes in to breakfast, having decided that he wants to invest the insurance money in Willy's scheme. First, however, Walter knows he must overcome the objections of his devout mother, Mama, who wants nothing to do with a liquor store and who has other plans for the money. Walter has decided to persuade Ruth to approach Mama on his behalf.

Looking at the play as a whole, we see that Walter has a deep overall need to win respect and self-esteem. He has chosen the objective of starting a liquor store as the action he hopes will satisfy that need. In this particular scene, that larger objective takes the immediate form of persuading Ruth to intercede with Mama.

Ruth, however, resists. Walter tries several strategies to win her over, each of which is a separate *unit of action,* or *beat:* He tries *to make her feel guilty* by reminding her that he missed a similar opportunity once before; he tries *to shame her* into "supporting her man"; and he *pleads* with her to save him from his despair. Each of these specific actions is driven by his need to win her over, and that need, in turn, is driven by his deep need to win self-esteem. (In terms we will explore further in later steps, Walter's *beat objectives* are strategies driven by his *scene objective,* which, in turn, is driven by his *superobjective.*)

Ruth, for her part, is driven by the need to deal with her secret pregnancy, which at this point she plans to terminate. She mistrusts Walter's friends (with good reason) and dislikes the shady aspects of Walter's scheme, which involves bribing city officials. What she most emphatically does *not* need at this moment is to be drawn into one of his harebrained schemes. Thus, her needs are in direct conflict with Walter's needs, a common and effective dramatic situation, and she finally explodes as she tells him, "Then go to work," which has the subtextual meanings of "Stop your whining," "Do the right thing," and "Leave me alone!"

You see that in each instance, the need is *internal* (inside the character) while the objective is *external* ("out there" in the other character). The need causes each character to form an objective, which is then pursued through a strategic action directed toward the other character. We say "strategic" action because the action chosen is one the character thinks will succeed; it is a strategy aimed at achieving the objective. In Walter's case, when trying to make Ruth feel guilty fails, he switches to shaming her, and then to pleading. In this case none of these strategies work.

Each character's action is a conduit through which energy flows from need toward objective, and when that action collides with the energy of the other character, it provokes a response in him or her, and so the scene moves forward, interaction by interaction. As you become more experienced with this way of working, you will sometimes be able to recognize beat changes as you read a scene; this early analysis of the structure of a scene is called a **breakdown**, or **scenario**. The technique of breaking a scene down will be explored in greater detail in Step 14, but for now you can begin to feel the rhythm and shape of your scene on a basic level.

EXERCISE 10.3: BREAKING DOWN THE SCENE

1. Working with your partner, come to a mutual agreement about where the overall crisis of the scene occurs.
2. Make a rough breakdown of the scene by identifying the units of action within it.
3. Define your character's action and objective in each beat. Remember to express each action as a transitive verb that is SIP, and think of each objective as a desired change in the other character.
4. Rehearse the scene together to emphasize and clarify its rhythms and the beat changes. Move so as to physicalize the beat changes by shifting your positions in relation to one another, but again, do not worry about blocking.

5. Carrying your script in hand, perform the scene in front of your group; ask the group members to note where they feel the beats changing and where they feel the crisis of the entire scene to be. Afterward, compare their responses to your scenario.

THE GIVEN CIRCUMSTANCES

Psychologists say that personality is shaped by both nature and nurture. Think of the ways your own personality has been shaped both by your genetic inheritance (your nature) and by the world in which you grew up (your nurture). Every day you interact with your world. It has physical, psychological, and social aspects that profoundly influence your feelings and thoughts. In reaction to these experiences, your personality is continuing to change and evolve in the direction established by your nature.

A character in a play or film has been given a nature by the author, who may even tell us something of the character's personal background as it was prior to the beginning of the play—commonly called the character's *backstory*. But the character is also shaped by nurture, by his or her interaction with the world created by the author, a world created specifically to serve the story and the character. As an actor, then, you must not only work on the inner qualities of your character, but also strive to experience the character's world and let your characterization develop within it. The specific qualities of the character's world are called the *given circumstances*. These **givens** fall into three categories: *who*, *where*, and *when*. Let's briefly examine each.

Who

Because personality is formed and influenced by our interactions with those around us, your character can be fully understood only by examining the *relationships* between him or her and all the other characters, whether they are physically present in your scene or not. These relationships have two aspects: the *general* and the *specific*. The general relationship provides basic considerations that make a relationship similar to others of its kind, whereas the specific relationship reveals what is unique to this particular case.

For example, in *Death of a Salesman*, Willy has a general relationship with his neighbor Charley. Like many neighbors, they talk about their work and their families and even give each other advice. But Willy and Charley also have a specific relationship that is very important to the overall meaning of the play. Charley is an easygoing man who, unlike Willy, has strong self-esteem. Charley advises Willy to accept himself and his life and be thankful for all he has. He even offers Willy a job, one that Willy's pride will not allow him to accept. In all, Charley represents a worldview that, if Willy could adopt it, might save his life.

Charley is sharply contrasted with Willy's brother Ben, who lives like a ghost in Willy's mind. Ben is the ultimate embodiment of the American Dream. Like the popular folk hero Horatio Alger, he tells Willy to "go West" and seek his fortune. One of the most important scenes in the play occurs when Willy is playing cards with Charley while at the same time talking to the image of Ben.

This scene shows us Willy being torn between the two ways of life embodied by Charley and Ben, neither of which he can really accept because of his deep-seated insecurity. At the end of the play, we see the contrast of Charley and Ben carried on in Willy's sons. Happy declares, "He had a good dream. It's the only dream you can have—to come out number-one man." But Biff says only, "I know who I am, kid." All of these characters can be fully understood only within their general and specific relationships.

Where

Where the play happens has two main aspects: the physical and the social. The *physical* environment has a tremendous influence on the action. For example, Shakespeare chose to set a play of great passion, *Othello*, in the hot and humid climate of Cyprus, whereas his play of intrigue and indecision, *Hamlet*, is properly set in the cold and isolated climate of Denmark. Likewise, the urban setting and the terribly cramped quarters of the apartments in *A Raisin in the Sun* and *The Glass Menagerie* embody Walter's and Tom's feelings of being trapped in a life over which they have no control.

The *social* environment is also of great importance. We've already mentioned the importance of the American Dream in these latter two plays; the values of the working class are fundamental in them. In *Zoot Suit,* the hysteria over World War II gives free rein to an innate prejudice against Mexican Americans, and the prideful culture of the Pachucos serves to inflame the confrontation. Similarly, the social climate of the bar in which *Cheers* is set is very much a character in the show. It is a home away from home, a place "where everybody knows your name." Here the characters share their most intimate feelings and problems, as Diane and Carla do in our sample scene (see Appendix A). In this scene, the spunky, street-tough, lower-class Carla freely shares her feelings with her co-worker, the classy, beautiful, but neurotic Diane. Carla's boyfriend, Ben Ludlow, is an eminent psychotherapist who is attracted to Carla because she is the only one in the bar who *doesn't* treat him with reverence. As in any good dramatic writing, each of the characters in *Cheers* was developed in relationship to all the others. Diane, for example, is the outsider who is a "fish out of water" in the world of *Cheers*, but she and the denizens of the bar gradually learn to relate to one another despite their great differences. In our sample scene, we see her even giving heartfelt advice to the tough Carla.

Minor characters, like Ben Ludlow in our sample scene and Bobo in *A Raisin in the Sun*, are usually given virtually no history and limited delineation. We might know only that one is an eminent psychologist, another a small, frightened, unsuccessful businessman. It is up to the actor to flesh these characters out in a way that is interesting, believable, appropriate to their function, and with a sense of economy that does not distract from the main story.

When

When a scene is happening is important in terms of the *time of day* and the *season. Death of a Salesman* begins in the summer—the season of warmth, growth, and fulfillment—and ends in the fall—the season of cold, decay, and impending death.

The *historical period* of a play—with all its implications for manners, values, and beliefs—is another important aspect of "when." Most of *The Glass Menagerie* is a memory of the 1930s, before World War II, and Tom tells us in his first speech that the Great Depression and "labor disturbances" at home and civil unrest overseas are "the social background of the play." We have already mentioned the importance of World War II to *Zoot Suit. A Raisin in the Sun* is set in the years after World War II, when many African American men returned from the war and an integrated army only to find that racism still oppressed them at home. *Cheers* is set in the present, but the bar has a timeless quality. It is a refuge from the real world, and so the producers were careful to avoid many of the issues and current news events that other television shows often use for plot material.

Older plays, or plays set in the past or other cultures, may present givens that are foreign to you, and some research will be required. In period plays, knowledge of the history, architecture, painting, music, religion, politics, and fashion of the time can be very useful. Even contemporary plays may involve circumstances and language that are unfamiliar to you.

To sum up, here is a list of the givens:

1. Who
   a. General relationships
   b. Specific relationships
2. Where
   a. Physical environment
   b. Social environment
3. When
   a. Time of day
   b. Season
   c. Historical period

Each of these given circumstances must be evaluated as to its relative importance; don't waste thought and energy on aspects of a character's world that do not contribute to the action and meaning of the play.

When possible, actually experiencing the most important givens can be a great help in rehearsing a scene. Consider working in locations that approximate the conditions of the scene. For example, I have several times held rehearsals for Shakespeare's *A Midsummer Night's Dream* in the woods at night by lantern light, because the sense memory of this experience greatly enriches the stage performance. In the same spirit, a director friend once forbid anyone in his cast to speak to the actor playing an alienated character, even outside rehearsals.

A note of caution: Beginning actors sometimes try to "indicate" the givens. Remember that it is not your job to *show* the audience anything about the character's world. Your job is simply to *live* in that world and let it affect you.

EXERCISE 10.4: THE GIVENS

1. Working with your partner, analyze the given circumstances of your scene, and discuss the influence of each on your character and on the action.
2. Rehearse the scene in ways that help you to experience the influence of the givens. For example, you might rehearse in a place that provides similar conditions to those of the play.
3. Carrying your script in hand, perform your scene for your group. Try to experience the givens as fully as possible.
4. Afterward, discuss with the group the sense of the givens they got from your performance and the influence of the givens on the scene. Did you avoid indicating the givens?

Summary of Step 10

The fundamental shape of rise, crisis, and release is the same on each of the several levels on which action operates: The individual interactions between characters work together to form the units of action we call beats, each of which has a minicrisis. The beats work together to form a scene, which has a crisis of its own, and the scenes flow together to lead us to the main crisis of the entire story.

A character is created in relationship to other characters and within a particular world. These given circumstances (who, where, and when) are essential to a proper understanding and experience of the character.

Summary of Part Two

External actions (sayings and doings) are driven by an urgent and immediate need to perform an action to achieve an objective that will fulfill that need. All external actions on stage need to be justified by the inner need that causes the external action. Your involvement in the action naturally produces emotion and character, not the other way around; you start with the doing and evolve toward the inner life that justifies it.

The Magic If allows your I to flow naturally into the new me of the created character. If you live in the world of the character and if you need what the character needs and if you do the things the character does to try to satisfy those needs, you naturally start to experience the life of the character and to modify your behavior and thought accordingly. This is the same process of give-and-take that develops your personality in real life.

Your focus on your objective allows you to become so engrossed in your action that you achieve public solitude and reduce self-consciousness, while your childlike capacity for dual consciousness allows your awareness to be simultaneously on your character's objective and on your artistic concerns as an actor. Finally, we say that your job is to do what the character does, completely and as if for the first time, with the precise qualities required, and is not to show us the character or his or her feelings by indicating. You do all of this in order to fulfill the dramatic function of your character within the play.

The best focus of awareness for an actor is the character's objective (what he or she wants), from which flows the character's action (what he or she does to try to get it). This focus on a single objective at the moment of action will overcome self-consciousness and give you power and control. Objectives become more effective when they are SIP: singular, immediate, and personal. Actions are best defined actively, using a simple verb phrase in transitive form. The inner needs that drive outer actions, including needs that must be expressed indirectly, are called a subtext.

A scene lives because of the energy flowing from character to character as they interact through the flow of action and reaction, which moves the scene forward and eventually creates the unfolding of the entire story. Action has both an internal and an external form; we think of a single flow of action that has both an inner phase and an outer phase.

In a well-structured play, an inciting incident establishes a fundamental conflict, followed by episodes of rising conflict and suspense, which lead to a crisis that is followed by a resolution in the climax. The individual interactions between characters work together to form the units of action we call beats, which work together to form a scene. The scenes flow together to lead us to the main crisis of the entire story. Analyzing the structure of a scene by identifying the beats is called doing a breakdown.

A character is created in relationship to other characters and within a particular world. These given circumstances (who, where, and when) are essential to a proper understanding and experience of the character.

PART THREE

Developing the Character

Having begun to prepare yourself to act and having come to a basic understanding of the concept of action, you can now begin to focus on the character you have chosen to create. You will begin by examining the script to form an initial understanding of the character's inner world, including the needs, thoughts, and choices that lie behind his or her actions. It is important that you understand that this analytical phase of your work on character is not the creation of a blueprint that is merely filled in during rehearsal. Rather, your initial analysis is intended to *inspire* and *guide* your exploration in rehearsal; it will point you in the direction you should go, but it will not determine the ultimate destination. Your actual performance will be discovered only gradually throughout your rehearsal process, when you begin to experience the give-and-take of the living event that will grow among you and your fellow workers. This process will be explored in Part 4.

11

The Character's
Traits and Needs

As we discussed in Part 1, your character was created to do a specific job within the scheme of the play as a whole. We called this the dramatic function of the character, and understanding this function will inspire and guide your work in rehearsal; too often actors approach their characters so personally that they begin to forget the larger purpose for which their characters were created. Without a larger sense of purpose, you might create a character who is alive and believable, but who doesn't do the intended job within the story as a whole. The audience might be impressed by such a performance, but the story would suffer and you would have failed in your main responsibility. According to Stanislavski, the actor's most important task is *to understand how every moment of the performance and every aspect of characterization contributes to the reason the play was written.*

The writer created the character so that he or she could believably perform the actions necessary to fulfill his or her dramatic function and gave the character certain traits that are consistent with those actions. Your work on your character begins with an examination of the traits established by the writer; these are the parameters within which you should work.

FUNCTION TRAITS

Characters are given certain traits that make their actions seem "natural." Aristotle called these *function traits* because they permit characters to believably fulfill their dramatic functions within a story. In *Death of a Salesman,* for example, Willy Loman is a man who, like many of his generation, measures his value as a human being by his success in his work. He is a man who sells; eventually we realize that he is selling himself. He feels that he is worthless until he persuades others, even his own sons, of his value, and he does this not only by making money, but also by earning the smiles and respect of his clients. Eventually, he makes the only "sale" he has left—his suicide enables his family to collect on his life insurance. We can say, then, that Willy's dramatic function is to represent the many people who are encouraged by our highly materialistic and competitive society to think that earning money and approval is the only source of self-esteem. Such people, like Willy, confuse material and spiritual values; and this, Miller is saying, can be a tragic consequence of the American Dream. Sadly, in our age of corporate downsizing and outsourcing, and at a time when entire professions are being made obsolete by technology, we see many people in Willy Loman's situation.

A Raisin in the Sun by Lorraine Hansberry is also a play about the American Dream. The title of the play refers to a poem by Langston Hughes in which unfulfilled dreams shrivel up "like a raisin in the sun." Every member of the Younger family has a dream, and Walter, like Willy Loman, wants to win self-esteem by making money. As he tells his wife, "I got to take hold of this here world, baby!" His scheme to open a liquor store is driven by his sense of failure: All he has to give his sons "is stories about how rich white people live. . . ." He is so driven that, like Willy Loman, he makes misguided choices. By the end of the play, however, it is Mama's dream of a home of their own that prevails because it will unite the family; they will risk fighting racial discrimination because they believe they can succeed if they stick together. Each member of the Younger family has a central function trait: Walter is desperate to feel like a worthy father, Beneatha wants to find and fulfill her own identity by serving the world meaningfully, and Mama wants to bind her family together.

In its own way, *Zoot Suit* by Luis Valdez also examines the American Dream. Henry Reyna wants to be treated with dignity and respect and is prone to self-destructive rage when he isn't. He and his family face a choice similar to that facing the Younger family in *A Raisin in the Sun*: how best to live authentically and combat the forces of discrimination. Some of the characters in *Zoot Suit*—especially Henry's alter ego, El Pachuco—urge defiance and even violence; others urge assimilation into the white culture; and still others urge a retreat into the family and ethnic tradition. The ultimate choice is not as important, Valdez would say, as confronting the discrimination that makes such a choice necessary.

In Tennessee Williams's *The Glass Menagerie*, Tom longs for the freedom to pursue his own life and thereby to discover his own identity. He is held back by his sense of obligation to his family, especially to his disabled sister. He is "the man of the house" and fears that if he leaves, it will be very hard for Laura and Amanda to get by. His only hope, then, is to find a replacement "man of the house" for Laura. Jim the gentleman caller is that hope, and it is a bitter irony that Jim fails to fulfill that hope because he is himself consumed by another example of the American Dream gone wrong. As he tells Laura:

> *Knowledge* – Zzzzzp! *Money* – Zzzzzzp! – *Power*! That's the cycle democracy is built on!

In each of these cases, the playwright has provided central function traits that drive the major characters to behave in ways that serve their stories—Willy Loman's insecurity, Walter Younger's ambition to "beat the system," Henry Reyna's angry need for respect and a sense of belonging, and Tom Wingfield's need to escape his obligations in search of his own identity; all are the main motivating forces that make the events of the plays seem natural and even inevitable.

RECOGNITION TRAITS

At a deep level, all of the characters we have mentioned are driven by fundamental human needs like the desire for self-esteem, love, or security. Drama, after all, portrays universal patterns of human experience that we can all recognize and share, and function traits are usually universal in this way. There is another kind of trait, however, that well-drawn characters must possess. According to Aristotle in *The Poetics*, we must be able to recognize characters as fellow human beings, even if we do not like them. A performance must therefore include traits that round out the character and make us recognize him or her as a real and specific human being who is in some way like us or like people we know or know about. We call these *recognition traits*, which are usually more specific to an individual character and less universal than function traits.

Arthur Miller tells us, for example, that Willy's wife loves him in spite of "his mercurial nature, his temper, his massive dreams and little cruelties." Miller also shows us that Willy tries hard to be fun with his male friends and is a bit of a flirt with the women. His mercurial nature makes him quick to anger but just as quick to be remorseful and apologetic. His great pride may sometimes drive him to be cruelly demeaning to others, as in his contempt for Charley's son Bernard. All these traits help to round out Willy as a recognizable human being.

Although some recognition traits are provided by a writer, this is an area in which an actor may contribute personal touches to a role that make it his or her own unique creation. For example, the actor might create physical and vocal traits that help round out the character: Willy might be a bit of a dandy in the way he dresses and carries himself in scenes from his earlier life, but he might be so disheartened later in life that he has let himself go, in both body and dress. When Dustin Hoffman played him, Willy had even developed a quivering hand and lip. There are many such recognition traits an actor might give Willy, some of which might be surprising—people, after all, are complex. But whatever traits the actor may contribute out of his own personality and imagination must never be allowed to obscure Willy's main function trait of profound insecurity.

As you prepare to rehearse, you should learn all you can about the character from the evidence within the text itself. The basic traits to look for are these:

1. Physical traits such as the character's age, body type, and any special physical traits or skills
2. Social traits such as his or her culture and historical period, social and economic class, educational background, and family background

3. Psychological traits such as intelligence, quickness, sensitivities, obsessions, or phobias

4. Moral traits such as beliefs and values, including religious and political views

Look not only at any character descriptions provided by the writer, but also at traits implied by action and things said about the character by other characters (remembering that their views may be biased). If there isn't much information supplied by the writer, it may be useful for you to invent some for yourself, although you must be careful to do this in a manner that supports and extends the character's function and qualities as determined by the author.

EXERCISE 11.1: INVENTORY OF CHARACTER TRAITS

Examine the evidence in the script about your character's traits.

1. Make a list that summarizes his or her physical, social, psychological, and moral traits.
2. Write a day-in-the-life diary entry in the character's own voice.

Remember that all this basic information about the character's traits is intended only to inspire and guide your exploration in rehearsal; you must not simply "put it on" as if it were a mask or costume. You will have to discover the inner world of the character that brings these traits to life—that is, the inner thoughts that lie behind the external actions—and in the process you will begin to find that new version of yourself that will be your special way of playing the role. This is what Stanislavski meant by the process of *transformation*. It will be the greatest creative and personal contribution you will make to your performance and the foundation of all the other work you will do on the role.

NEEDS AND PERSONALIZATION

Like your own behavior in everyday life, your character's behavior is driven by needs. One of the best ways to personalize your sense of the character, to make it your own, is to identify the character's needs and experience them for yourself or find analogous needs in your own experience. You should begin by examining the script, analyzing the character's actions and speech, and then work backward to deduce his or her needs.

You can see that we come to understand a character's needs through his or her actions. Actors sometimes make the mistake of trying to "play" needs: They try to *show* us how much they need self-esteem, how much they need to be left alone, and so on. But as you already know, this results in *indicating*—that is, *showing* instead of *doing*. Trust that the writer has constructed the character so that his or her actions spring naturally from his or her needs. It will be much more satisfying for audience members to figure out those needs for themselves, rather than have you show them what they are.

EXERCISE 11.2: NEEDS

1. Examine the entire play from which your scene comes: Does your character have some deep-seated, overall need that drives his or her actions throughout the play?

2. How does this one overall need manifest itself within your scene? What are the immediate and specific needs driving your character within this scene?

3. Read through the scene with your partner. Do the needs of your characters conflict with each other? How can you maximize this conflict?

4. Do you have needs that are similar to those of your character? Can you begin to imagine yourself in the character's place, needing the same or analogous things?

You possess a vast personal potential. If you can engage your own energy in your character's actions within the scripted world and can make that world and those actions real for yourself, even if they are unfamiliar, you will find yourself naturally transformed into a new state of being. In other words, acting is as much *self-expansion* as it is *self-expression*. This expansion, this exploration of new states of being, is the most exciting aspect of the actor's creative process.

EMOTION RECALL AND SUBSTITUTION

If you encounter a character whose needs or circumstances are so unfamiliar that you have difficulty experiencing them, you might try two techniques designed to help you connect material from your own life to your work. These techniques are ***emotion recall*** and ***substitution***.

Stanislavski experimented with the idea that an actor could develop a wealth of emotion memories as a resource for the acting process, much as a painter learns to mix colors:

> The broader your emotion memory, the richer your material for inner creativeness. . . . Our creative experiences are vivid and full in direct proportion to the power, keenness and exactness of our memory. . . . Sometimes memories continue to live in us, grow and become deeper. They even stimulate new processes and either fill out unfinished details or suggest altogether new ones.[1]

There are several techniques by which stored memories may be recalled. One of the easiest of these techniques is ***visualization,*** which involves relaxing deeply and imagining yourself in the character's world, with all its sights,

---

[1]Constantin Stanislavski, *An Actor's Handbook*, trans. and ed. Elizabeth Reynolds Hapgood (New York: Theatre Arts Books, 1936), p. 56. Copyright © 1936, 1961, 1963 by Elizabeth Reynolds Hapgood.

sounds, smells, physical sensations, and so on. Imagine yourself in your character's situation with all the feelings and needs it involves. From these imagined experiences, you can invite associations from your store of personal memories. These associations, or *recalls,* automatically become attached to the character's actions and situation. It is neither necessary nor desirable to "play" them; simply allow them to influence you.

The key to this technique is relaxation. When we relax, our storehouse of memory and subconscious material becomes more accessible. You may notice that when you do relaxation exercises such as meditation, memories often naturally flood in.

Another technique that may be useful in certain situations involves making a mental *substitution* of some situation or person from your own life for the situation or character in the scene. If, for example, you are expected to be terribly afraid of another character, it might be useful to recall some frightening person from your own life and substitute that person in your own mind for the other character. Such a substitution will often arise naturally as you form associations between the world of the character and your own experience.

Of course, such emotion recalls and substitutions need not be rooted in real events; fantasy sometimes supplies more powerful material than real life does. Your dreams and imagination already provide a storehouse of situations and characters that are as useful in your acting as anything from your real life.

A word of caution, however: As useful as emotion recalls and substitutions may sometimes be, they can also be dangerous. First, memories can be very powerful and can *overwhelm artistic control.* Second, recalls and substitutions can become *obstacles between you and your scene partners;* it is awful to be on stage with someone who is looking at you with a vacant stare because he or she is "seeing" someone else in his or her own mind or is busy reliving the day the family dog died. Third, and most dangerous, the emotional power of recalls may distract you from your focus on your objective and may lure you into *playing an emotional state.* For all these reasons, recalls and substitutions may be carefully used in rehearsal but are absolutely *not* intended for use in performance. Stanislavski himself eventually abandoned these techniques entirely.

EXERCISE 11.3: PERSONALIZATION

1. Place yourself comfortably at rest, and take a few deep breaths to relax.
2. Now go through your scene mentally; picture the entire circumstance, and live through your character's actions as if you were actually doing them in those circumstances. Let your body respond freely. (This technique, used by Olympic athletes with great success, is called **visuo-motor behavior rehearsal** [VMBR] and will be covered in detail in Step 16.)
3. As you live through the scene in your mind, notice the emotional associations that arise. Do you remember events from your past? Do the other characters remind you of people you have known? Let yourself relive these memories fully.

4. Review this exercise, and evaluate any connections that were made. Are they useful to the scene? Do they need to be altered to meet the exact demands of the scene?

5. Perform your scene (with script in hand) in front of your group. Allow these associations to influence you, but avoid indicating them.

6. After your performance, discuss it with the group. Were you able to endow your character's need, situation, and action with personal significance? Did the character seem more real to the group? Are you beginning to feel a transformation into the character?

Summary of Step 11

A writer creates a character to believably perform the actions necessary to fulfill his or her dramatic function and gives the character certain traits that are consistent with those actions. Your work on your character begins with an examination of the traits established by the writer; these are the parameters within which you should work. Characters are given certain traits that make their actions seem "natural." Aristotle called these function traits because they permit characters to believably fulfill their dramatic functions within a story.

There is another kind of trait that well-drawn characters must also possess. According to Aristotle in *The Poetics*, we must be able to recognize characters as fellow human beings, even if we do not like them. A performance must therefore include traits that round out the character and make us recognize him or her as a real and specific human being who is in some way like us or like people we know or know about. We call these recognition traits, which are usually more specific to an individual character and less universal than function traits. Although some recognition traits are provided by a writer, this is an area in which an actor may contribute personal touches to a role that make it his or her own unique creation. Function and recognition traits can be of four main types: physical, social, psychological, and moral.

An important part of your job is to experience your character's needs as if they were your own. You do this by personalizing the character's needs, putting yourself in his or her place and making the character's needs and experiences your own. Besides your natural ability to empathize with your character, there are several techniques that can help in this effort, such as recalling emotional experiences or substituting relationships from your own life. These techniques may be part of your personal preparation, but they are *not* meant to be used in performance because they may distance you from the scene and your partners.

12 Getting into the Character's Mind

L et's review our basic premise about how action flows in a scene; think back to the Impulse Circle exercise (9.1). The slap you received was a **stimulus**—it aroused you, caused a *reaction* as it passed through you, and then left you as an *action* as you slapped the next person's hand. Your action then became a stimulus for the next person and generated a reaction, which in turn generated another action, and so the slap moved around the circle. Similarly, a dramatic scene moves as the characters react to and act with one another. As in the impulse circle, reaction turns into action and produces the flow of action–reaction–action–reaction that moves the story forward.

The impulse circle was not exactly like a scene, of course. In the exercise, the slap was more or less the same as it moved around the circle, which would become repetitive and boring after a while. In a dramatic scene, the energy leaving each character as action is not the same as the energy that enters as stimulus; as it passes through each character, it is altered by his or her needs, personality, and objectives. So in a scene on stage, the "slap" is continually changing as the story evolves, which makes it more interesting and suspenseful.

From this example, you can see that each character is a channel through which the energy of the story flows and that each character contributes something special to the changing nature of that energy as the story unfolds. *The inner thought process of each character is designed to produce the proper effect on each link of the reaction–action flow.* In this step you will explore what happens inside your character moment by moment as his or her reaction to a stimulus turns into an action directed toward an objective, as needed at that moment to move the story forward properly. As these discoveries accumulate and are experienced during the rehearsal process, they naturally begin to move you toward transformation.

When we examine the inner thought process that leads to an action, we see that it consists of several steps. For example, think of the moment in *Death of a Salesman* when Willy enters and sees Howard playing with the recorder. What Willy sees is his *stimulus*, and the act of seeing it is his *perception*. This stimulus *arouses* Willy and prompts an *attitude* toward it; he is impatient because the recorder is distracting Howard from listening to him. Willy considers what to do; we'll call this his *deliberation*. There are several possible courses of action; with one he could interrupt Howard and ask that Howard listen to him, but this might alienate Howard. Willy's experience as a salesman tells him that he can use the recorder to advantage by ingratiating himself to Howard, and so Willy makes a *strategic choice*: He pretends to admire the recorder. Thus, praising the recorder in order to gain Howard's favor becomes Willy's *action*, directed toward his *objective,* which is to ingratiate himself to Howard and thereby get his attention.

This example illustrates the internal process by which action is formed: You *perceive a stimulus* that arouses you and generates an *attitude,* which prompts a *consideration of alternatives* and leads to a *strategic choice* of an *action* directed toward an *objective*. This thought process is represented graphically in Figure 12.1. In this figure, the large circle represents your skin, the boundary between your inner world and the outer world. The stimulus enters you through your perception (seeing, hearing, touching). It arouses a response in you that carries some attitude—it may excite or frighten or please or anger you. At this point, your action may be automatic, or deliberation may generate a strategic choice. The chosen action may then be *direct, indirect,* or *suppressed.* By fully reliving this inner phase of your character's action, you will most effectively enter into the character's mind. Let's explore each step of this process in detail.

PERCEPTION, AROUSAL, AND ATTITUDE

The process of inner action must begin with real perception, real hearing and seeing. Although this seems obvious, some actors only pretend to hear or see what is said or done to them; they fear that if they let the other characters truly affect them, they will lose control of their performances. Instead of trusting and opening up to the other actors, they prefer the safety of reacting only to their own idea of what they want the other characters to say and do. It is as if they are responding to a prerecorded, premeditated image of the other actor inside their own heads. When this happens, the performance becomes false and mechanical. Don't let fear turn you into this kind of hermetically sealed actor.

Actors have to depend on each other to provide what they and the scene need moment by moment to move the story forward as a real human event. Each actor must supply the required stimuli, and each must truly receive the stimuli provided. Although this doesn't always happen, we strive to achieve this ideal working relationship of real giving and taking. Remember: Acting is not so much doing things as it is allowing yourself to be *made* to do them. *Real acting is real reacting!* As you work, ask yourself, Am I really hearing and seeing my partner, or am I anticipating what I want him or her to say or do?

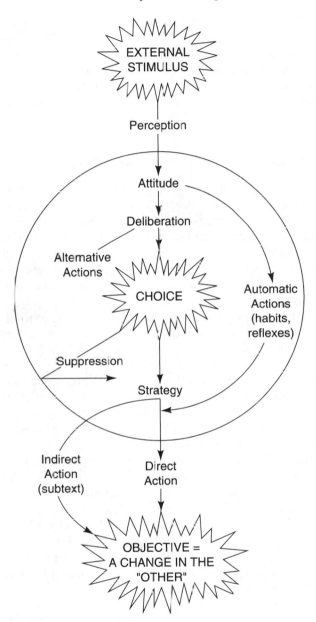

FIGURE 12.1 The Inner Process of Action.

Once a stimulus has been truly perceived, it gets inside you and arouses you. This arousal has a certain quality that we will call your *attitude*. Ask yourself, What does this mean to me? How do I feel about it? Of course, beware of indicating your attitude; simply allow yourself to respond to the stimulus, and allow it to arouse you in this way as if for the first time.

Once we are aroused, it is human nature to try to do something that will resolve the arousal. Psychologists call this the need for *homeostasis*; it is profoundly uncomfortable to remain in a state of arousal without doing something about it, even if it is to try to ignore the arousal by suppressing it (a strategy that has dire consequences, as in the case of Hamlet). But whether suppressed or not, the arousal energizes us, and we are motivated to take further action through either unconscious or conscious processes.

AUTOMATIC AND SPONTANEOUS ACTIONS

As in real life, dramatic characters sometimes act out of habit or impulse; in such cases, the stimulus leads directly to external action without conscious thought (see the arrow bypassing CHOICE in Figure 12.1). This is what Stanislavski called **automatic** action. When the slap in the Impulse Circle exercise was moving quickly, it became an automatic action, something you did without thinking. Likewise, some of the things your character does will be done automatically or unconsciously. In everyday life, we call this unconscious and automatic behavior *habit*.

When you are approaching a part, it is extremely useful to identify the habitual aspects of your character's behavior as soon as possible. You will want to strive to recreate the character's habits in yourself (only for purposes of playing the role, of course). Much of the behavior of characters may be habitual, things that they have been doing all their lives and that are "built into" them: their voice, walk, mannerisms, any special skills (like swordsmanship or knowing how to move in a hoop skirt). Through repeated rehearsal and homework, these habits should become as natural to you as they are to your character. This takes time, and there is no substitute for practice.

Besides these habits, there is another type of automatic action: Your character may experience important moments in which he or she is caught unawares by something and reacts *spontaneously*—as in moments of surprise or shock, or moments when the character suddenly understands or recognizes something. For example, in the sample scene from *Cheers* in Appendix A, Carla begins with a vague feeling that she cannot marry Ben Ludlow, but she does not know exactly why. At first she thinks it is because he won't want her once he knows the truth about her children, but she soon discovers that he is willing to accept that. And yet she can't bring herself to say yes.

LUDLOW: I still haven't heard you say yes.

CARLA: I know. [*Genuinely puzzled*] Why do you think that is?

LUDLOW: I think if you examine your feelings, you'll know.

CARLA: Yeah, I guess I know. I love somebody else.

Just before Carla says, "Yeah, I guess I know," she has what Aristotle called a **recognition** about the "dream man" in her mind. For Carla this has to be a moment of spontaneous self-insight; such moments cannot be mechanically recreated and must happen afresh every time they are performed. In a sense, you have to forget what you are going to discover and then let yourself find it anew. This does not mean, however, that the form of the moment will vary wildly; you can learn to let it happen within parameters that serve the performance.

EXERCISE 12.1: AUTOMATIC ACTION ANALYSIS

Review your scene with your partner.

1. Does your character have any habitual traits? What do these things tell you about your character? What can you do to develop these habits in yourself for this role?
2. Are there moments of recognition, surprise, or impulse that must be spontaneous?

DELIBERATION AND STRATEGIC CHOICE

In Figure 12.1 you see that if an action is not automatic, a conscious process of thought begins. The first step in this conscious process is to consider various things you might do. During this **deliberation**, one course of action is chosen, and others are rejected. In order to fully experience this process, it may be useful to create the alternative choices that your character rejects. These can only be implied by the writer, and you must flesh them out for yourself using your growing understanding of the character and the character's circumstances. This can be your own special way of personalizing the character's inner world and can help you fully experience each choice your character makes. After all, you can't really live through a choice unless you have real alternatives from which to choose. In other words, it may be as important for you to decide what your character chooses *not* to do as it is to know what he or she *does*. Even after you have created the alternatives, you must be sure to live through the choice anew every time you perform it, or it may start to become automatic.

Having deliberated the alternatives, your character—like people in everyday life—makes the choice that he or she thinks has the best chance for success, given the circumstances. We call this a **strategic choice**. The strategy is formed mainly in relationship to the other characters and what your character thinks will elicit the best response from them. For example, in *Death of a Salesman,* Willy finds Howard playing with his recorder. As a seasoned salesman, Willy knows how to get his foot in the door by feigning interest in the recorder and even praising the inane recording of the family. This strategy seems like the best chance to achieve Willy's real objective, to get Howard's attention so he can ask for a spot in town.

Follow the flow of energy in Figure 12.1, and notice that strategic choice is at the center of the entire inner process. Before the choice, energy is moving *into* you; after the choice, energy is moving *out* of you. In other words, *choice is the point at which reaction turns into action*—the essence of drama. The most suspenseful moments in stories occur when a character confronts a significant and difficult choice and we wonder, What will he or she do?

Choice is also the most revealing and expressive point in the process of action. In the making of significant choices, your character is influenced by his or her needs, ways of seeing the world, relationships, beliefs, and values. *If you can experience all the factors influencing your character's most significant choices, you will be in touch with everything needed to create the character's mind.*

Your experience of your character's significant choices is also the main way the Magic If produces transformation in you. When you have entered into your character's circumstances and felt his or her needs, and then have truly lived through his or her choices, action will follow naturally, and with it will come transformation.

Of course, not every choice your character makes is to be given the weight of the significant choices we have been discussing here. In a typical scene, there will be only one or two such significant choices; in an entire role, there may be one singular choice that stands out above all the rest. In the scene from *Cheers,* for example, Carla's main choice is to not marry Ben, whereas Ben's main choice is to accept Carla's rejection with grace. Everything that is said and done in the scene either leads to or flows from these two crucial choices.

THE INNER MONOLOGUE

Experiencing the process whereby your character forms his or her actions is the most important step toward transformation. Here is a good general rule: Whatever your character *doesn't* need to think about ideally should become automatic or spontaneous for you as well; whatever your character *does* need to think about, you must also think through each and every time you perform the scene.

As a detailed example of this process of inner action, consider this exchange between Amanda and Laura from a scene in *The Glass Menagerie.* Amanda has just discovered that her daughter has not been going to her classes at a business college; she is very upset because she had hoped Laura could have a business career, and she is thinking about what else Laura can do.

> AMANDA: Girls that aren't cut out for business careers usually wind up married to some nice man. *[She gets up with a spark of revival.]* Sister, that's what you'll do!
> *[Laura utters a startled, doubtful laugh. She reaches quickly for a piece of glass.]*
>
> LAURA: But, Mother—
>
> AMANDA: Yes? *[She goes over to the photograph.]*
>
> LAURA: *[In a tone of frightened apology]* I'm—crippled!

There are two significant choices made in this brief beat, one by each character. First, just before she *"gets up with a spark of revival,"* Amanda decides that she has to get Laura married. Her inner thought process in making this choice might flow like this:

1. ***Stimulus.*** Marriage! To some nice man! Of course!
2. ***Attitude.*** But I'll have to take charge, or nothing will happen.
3. ***Alternatives.*** She has no gentlemen callers the way I did. How can we find one?
4. ***Choice.*** Tom must know lots of nice young men down at the shoe factory.
5. ***Action.*** "Sister, that's what you'll do!"
6. ***Objective.*** To rally Laura to the plan.

When Laura hears her mother's idea, she reaches for the glass animal and goes over to the photograph of her father. These are automatic actions, things she does every time she feels threatened—a retreat into her "safe" illusory world. But she also tries to deal with the situation in a conscious way, and her internal thought process might flow like this:

1. ***Stimulus.*** Married? Can she really be thinking that?
2. ***Attitude.*** No one would want to marry me—I'm a cripple.
3. ***Alternatives.*** I could just hide (*reaching for the glass animal*). Or maybe I could run away, the way father did (*going to the photograph*).
4. ***Choice.*** No, I've got to talk her out of it.
5. ***Action.*** "But mother . . . I'm—crippled!"
6. ***Objective.*** To make mother see that her plan is impossible.

You can see that Amanda's and Laura's needs, values, way of thinking, sense of self, way of relating to the world—in short, their entire psychology—is involved and expressed in each step of their mental processes. Notice, too, how Tennessee Williams has provided physical actions (Amanda getting up and Laura going to the animals and photograph) that externalize the inner thought processes of both characters.

Giving words to the internal thought process in the way we just did is called creating an **inner monologue**. Purposefully creating such a detailed inner monologue as part of your preparation for a role can help you to specify and experience your understanding of your character's thought process. In performance, this thought process will once again become intuitive and nearly instantaneous.

Such a highly detailed view of your character's inner thought process may be useful for highly significant choices, but it is too cumbersome to use on a moment-by-moment basis. By simplifying the process, you can achieve an easy formula to apply as you rehearse. Break the process into three basic steps: The stimulus, need, and attitude form the first step, which we will call simply *arousal*; the consideration of alternatives and the choice of a strategic action become the second step, which constitutes the *choice*; finally, the external activity directed toward your objective is the *action*. So your inner process can be summarized by three key words:

arousal–choice–action

You can apply this system by asking yourself three questions about each of the transactions in a scene:

1. What am I reacting to?
2. What does it make me want?
3. What do I do to try to get it, and what *don't* I do?

EXERCISE 12.2: CHOICE ANALYSIS

1. Answer these three questions about each of your character's actions in your scene.
2. Choose the most significant choice your character makes in the scene, and examine it in detail. Create the inner monologue that expresses your character's mental process for this choice. Try writing down the inner monologue.
3. Rehearse your scene with your partner. Take the time to experience each choice fully.
4. Perform the scene (with script in hand) for your group, and discuss it. Were the moments of choice clear and believable?

By now, you are well on your way to having your scene memorized. *Subsequent exercises will require that you have your lines thoroughly memorized*. We call this getting **off book**. Begin now to get completely off book; have your partner or someone else cue you. You will find that the more fully you understand your character's actions, the easier it will be to learn your lines, which are driven by those actions.

Summary of Step 12

The internal process by which conscious action is formed looks like this: You perceive a stimulus that arouses you and generates an attitude, which prompts a consideration of alternatives, which leads to a strategic choice of an action directed toward an objective. The chosen action may be direct, indirect, or suppressed. By fully reliving this inner phase of action, you will most effectively enter into your character's mind.

Dramatic characters sometimes act out of habit or impulse, when a stimulus leads directly to external action without conscious thought; a character may also experience important moments in which he or she is caught unawares by something and reacts spontaneously. These are what Stanislavski called automatic actions. If an action is not automatic, it is the result of a process of deliberation and strategic choice. Strategic choice is at the center of the entire inner process; before the choice, energy is moving into you; after the choice, energy is moving out of you. Because choice is the moment at which reaction turns into action, it is the essence of drama.

Experiencing the process whereby your character forms his or her actions is the most important step toward transformation. Here is a good general rule:

Whatever your character *doesn't* need to think about ideally should become automatic or spontaneous for you as well; whatever your character *does* need to think about, you must also think through each and every time you perform the scene. Giving words to an internal thought process is called creating an inner monologue. Your inner process can be summarized by three key words: arousal–choice–action.

13

Exploring the Character's Language

O ne of the first things you will notice about a good play is the effectiveness of its language as an expression of the feeling and personality of the character who is speaking. The words of the dialogue are the "residue" of the character's total state of being as envisioned by the writer; an actor can enter into the character through those words. The old-fashioned acting adage "Just say the words" had some truth to it, though of course the words must be said with a full re-creation of the living process that produces them. Your study of your role, therefore, begins with respect for the details and implications of your character's language, which has been so carefully wrought by the author.

In everyday life, speech is the result of a process; you begin with a *germinal* idea or feeling, an impulse that needs to be formed into words, and you then choose the words that will best communicate to others. Although this *process of verbalization* usually happens almost instantaneously, complex thoughts and deep feelings sometimes require considerable effort to verbalize. A dramatic character on stage must go through this same process of verbalization, and you, the actor playing the character, must re-create and re-experience this process each and every time you speak your lines. This is the only way to keep your character's language alive, happening right now, as if before our eyes. If you fail to relive this process of word choice, your lines will inevitably sound mechanical and rehearsed. As good actors say, you must come to "own" the character's words as if they were your own by re-creating and re-experiencing the living process by which that language is formed. This requires working backward from the finished language provided by the writer to discover its genesis in the mind of the character. In this step, you will explore the clues within the character's language that can lead you to direct participation in the mind that produces that language.

WORD CHOICE

The critical moment in the process of verbalization occurs when characters choose the words they speak in order to communicate an idea, feeling, or desire. This word choice is called *diction* (a word sometimes used to mean "enunciation" but used here in its primary meaning, "choice of words to express ideas," as in *dictionary*). The words your character speaks have two kinds of meaning: their literal dictionary meanings, called **denotation**, and their implied emotional values, called **connotation**. We will consider denotation first.

Denotation

Denotation is not a static thing; there may be several possible definitions for a word, and the meaning of words in popular usage sometimes changes quickly. You must be sure that the meaning you take for granted today is not a distortion of the playwright's original intention. For example, Juliet, coming out on her balcony, says, "O Romeo, Romeo! Wherefore art thou Romeo?" Some young actresses deliver this line as if Juliet were wishing that Romeo were there, in the sense of "Romeo, where are you?" But when we discover that in Shakespeare's day *wherefore* meant 'why,' we see that she really is saying, "Why are you named Romeo, member of a family hated by my own?" Such obsolete meanings are sometimes labeled "archaic" in the dictionary.

Playwrights will sometimes manipulate denotation by *punning,* placing a word that has more than one denotation in a context in which both meanings could be applied. Although puns have been called the lowest form of humor, they may be used for both serious and comic effect. For example, when we examine the names of Beckett's characters in his play *Endgame*, we see that the name of the master "Hamm" reminds us of meat, while his servant "Clov" refers to the spice (clove) traditionally used with ham for flavor and preservation. But Beckett doesn't stop there; ham is meat that comes from an animal with a cloven hoof, and Clov does indeed act as the "feet" of Hamm, since Hamm cannot walk. There is also the "Ham actor," the tragedian, and Clov, the clown; and the overbearing Hamm (hammer) pounds down Clov (*ciou* means "nail" in French) as well as the other two characters in the play, Nagg and Nell (*nagel* means "nail" in German). All these multiple meanings are wonderfully appropriate to the play.

Characters in plays frequently use topical and *colloquial* speech, the highly informal, conversational language of a particular time and place. For example, calling a beautiful woman "a dish" or "a real tomato," or her legs "a pair of gams," summons up 1930s America in a very specific way. Colloquial words and phrases tend to change their meaning very quickly, and doing a play even ten years old may require some investigation of the meaning of words and expressions it contains. Good dictionaries will help you to be sure about denotation. For old plays, the *Oxford English Dictionary* (OED) lists the changing meanings of words with the dates of their currency. There are also carefully noted editions of great classical plays with glossaries and notes that are very helpful.

Connotation

Whereas denotation refers to the literal meaning of words, *connotation* is defined as "suggestive or associative implication of a term beyond its literal, explicit sense." The connotation of words can reveal the attitudes and feelings of a character. A dictionary will sometimes be helpful in giving examples of connotations, but the connotative possibilities of words are multiple and variable; the word *politic*, for example, is defined as "artful; ingenious; shrewd" but also as "crafty; unscrupulous; cunning." You need to consider the context in order to determine which of the connotative possibilities of a word are appropriate. When Shakespeare's King Lear speaks of "a scurvy politician," we know just how he feels about the man. Likewise, when Blanche DuBois in *A Streetcar Named Desire* describes Stanley Kowalski as "swilling and gnawing and hulking," we understand not only her attitude toward Stanley, but also something about Blanche herself because she has chosen to express her disgust in such vividly bodily ways. The physical qualities of "swilling and gnawing and hulking" invite the actress to participate in the sensations they evoke, and this physicalization of the language can provide a strong sense not only of Blanche's disgust for Stanley, but also her barely suppressed sexuality.

To sum up, your understanding of your lines depends on your understanding of their meaning and feeling in a historical, social, and psychological context. You must consider *the meanings of the words when the play was written* and *the feelings they express when used by this kind of character in this situation*. One very good way to be sure you have examined the meanings of your lines is to **paraphrase** the lines, restate them in your own words, as if you were doing a translation of the original. Obviously, much of the emotional tone and poetic richness of the original will be lost, but you will have ensured that you have considered seriously the possible values of each word you speak.

EXERCISE 13.1: PARAPHRASE ON THREE LEVELS

Using one of the more important speeches from your scene, write a paraphrase of it on each of the following levels:

1. To express as simply as possible the *germinal idea* behind each sentence
2. To express the literal denotation, word by word
3. To express the connotations and emotional attitudes by pushing the feelings to an extreme, using language that is natural to you

Try performing this last paraphrase.

RHYTHM

The rhythm of speech refers to its tempo (fast or slow), its underlying "beat" (regular or irregular, heavy or light), and the variations of tempo and beat that provide emphasis on certain words or other elements of the speech, thereby enhancing their meaning. Rhythm is highly expressive of personality; a blustery, pompous person has a rhythm of speech much different from that of a thought-ful, introspective person. Even nationality and social background affect rhythm; the Irish, for example, tend to speak each thought on one long exhalation of breath, imparting an unmistakable rhythm to their speech. Good playwrights build in the rhythms of speech that are appropriate to a character's personality and emotion, and your analysis of those rhythms will aid you in forming your characterization.

Many emotions have recognizable rhythmic implications. All emotion causes measurable changes in the tension of our muscles, and this tensing of the muscles has a direct effect on our speech. Take anger as an example: As anger rises in us, the body becomes tense, especially in the deep center, where our largest muscles mobilize themselves for action. This tension in the interior muscles is communicated directly to the diaphragm, limiting its movement and forcing us to take shallow breaths; but since we need to oxygenate our muscles for defense purposes, we compensate by taking more rapid breaths. These changes cause us to break up our speech into shorter breath phrases and to increase its tempo. Tension spreading to the pharynx causes an elevation of pitch, which, when coupled with the increased pressure of the breath stream, results in a "punching" delivery and increased volume. As the tension moves into the jaw, it encourages us to emphasize hard consonant sounds. As a result, our angry speech may become similar to the snapping and growling of an animal about to bite.

This very basic example shows you that both rhythm and tone are tied to your emotional state by the muscles that produce speech. Because playwrights and screenwriters know that their dialogue will be performed aloud by actors, they write with a special sensitivity to the effect the words will have on an actor. By understanding the rhythms and tones your playwright has supplied for you, and by experiencing them in your own muscles as you pronounce the words, you will have a chance to experience the feelings they express. An active physical participation in your character's language is a powerful tool for entering into the life of the character.

A skillful writer shapes rhythm on several levels at once. The fundamental rhythm is established by the flow of accented and unaccented syllables; we call this the **syllable cadence**. Look at the following example from Samuel Beckett's *Endgame*; you will see that Beckett has used rhythmic patterns of two and three syllables. Read the passage aloud for full rhythmic effect; tap your feet.

One day you'll be blind, like me. You'll be sitting there, a speck in the void, in the dark, forever, like me. (pause) One day you'll say to yourself, I'm tired. I'll sit down, and you'll go and sit down. Then you'll say, I'm hungry, I'll get up and get something to eat. But you won't get up. You'll say, I shouldn't have sat down, but since I have I'll sit on a little longer, then I'll get up and get something to eat. (pause) But you won't get up and you won't get anything to eat. (pause) And there you'll be, like a little bit of grit, in the middle of the steppe.

The rhythmic flow of these syllables is as highly developed as any formal poetry.

Another level of rhythm, the **breath cadence**, is of special importance to an actor. The evolution of our written language was greatly influenced by the physical act of speaking; we tend to divide our thoughts into sentences that can be said in one breath. When a thought is complex enough to require several phrases, we separate these into "sub-breaths" by commas, semicolons, or colons (in music the comma is still used as a breath mark). Playwrights manipulate breath cadences to guide an actor into a pattern of breathing, and the rhythm of breath is a primary factor in emotion. Try reading the Beckett piece aloud, taking a small breath at every comma, a full breath at each period, and a long breath at each "(pause)." What emotional experience results? Next, try the same experiment using the speech from your scene, which you paraphrased in Exercise 13.1.

Finally, the dialogue itself, as the characters speak one after another, has a rhythm. Each speech usually contains a central idea and functions in a way similar to that of paragraphs in prose; the alternation of the speeches creates the **dialogue cadence**. We get a good impression of the tempo of a scene by looking at the density of the printed script; a mass of long speeches suggests a different approach to tempo, for example, than does an extremely short back-and-forth exchange. You may notice, too, that changes in tempo and rhythm are suggested by a sudden change in the dialogue cadence, as when one character's very long speech is answered by a short response from the other, or when a scene breaks into a series of very short exchanges of shared or interrupted lines, which in classical drama is called **stichomythia**.

Here is a summary of these cadences, or levels of rhythm:

1. Syllable cadence
2. Breath cadence
3. Dialogue cadence

However, remember that the rhythm of speech does not absolutely determine meaning or even emotion; your choices must be based upon your understanding of the meaning of the lines, taking into account the demands of character and situation. Nevertheless, by recognizing the rhythms and sounds the writer has built into your character's speech, and by experiencing them fully in your own muscles, you will find them a powerful aid in entering into the consciousness of your character. As Stanislavski said:

> There is an indissoluble interdependence, interaction and bond between tempo-rhythm and feeling. . . . The correctly established tempo-rhythm of a play or a role can, of itself, intuitively (on occasion automatically) take hold of the feelings of an actor and arouse in him a true sense of living his part.[1]

---

[1] From Constantin Stanislavski, *Building a Character*, trans. Elizabeth Reynolds Hapgood (New York: Theatre Arts Books, 1949), pp. 218–236. Theatre Arts Books, 153 Waverly Place, New York, NY 10014.

THE MUSIC OF SPEECH

There is a story about the famous Italian actress Eleanora Duse. Her speech, it was said, was so emotionally rich that she once moved a New York audience to tears by reading from the Manhattan telephone book. True or not, the story shows that any good actor develops great expressiveness in the use of the music of speech, and playwrights are careful to provide language that is rich in its musical potential, whatever quality it may have, from the lyrical sweep of Tennessee Williams to the curt staccato of David Mamet.

There have been attempts to develop systems that attach certain meanings to certain linguistic sounds. The most famous of these was the **Roback Voco-Sensory Theory**. In one of his experiments, Roback's subjects were asked to tell which three-letter nonsense syllable, "mil" or "mal," made them think of larger or smaller objects. As you might guess, most subjects thought that "mal" meant something bigger than "mil." The theory points out that the physical act of saying "mal" requires opening the mouth more than does saying "mil," and this causes the sensation of bigness associated with "mal." The opposite is true for "mil," which is a "smaller" sound. The theory goes on to suggest that much of language was formed by the effect of the physical sensations of speaking: Rough words *feel* rough, and smooth words *feel* smooth, for example, just as *rushing* rushes, *explodes* explodes, and so on.

This theory has great limitations, however, since many words do not seem to relate to their physical qualities; for instance, *small* is made up of big sounds, while *big* is small. Nevertheless, the theory provides an interesting view of language for an actor since it encourages a way of speaking that emphasizes the relationship of physical sensation and the meaning and feeling of speech. Try reading the previous speech from Samuel Beckett's *Endgame* so as to emphasize its tonal values. Feel how Beckett has selected words whose sounds can be useful to you in supporting the meaning and emotional tone of the speech. Feel especially the shift from big, open vowel sounds in the main body of the speech (illustrated in the first example here) to the little, hard consonant sounds in the last line (repeated in the second example here):

> One day you'll be blind, like me. You'll be sitting there, a speck in the void, in the dark, forever, like me.
>   And there you'll be, like a little bit of grit, in the middle of the steppe.

Do you see how this shift can communicate a vivid experience of the isolation and insignificance the speaker feels?

Stanislavski, in *Building a Character,* sums it up this way:

> Letters, syllables, words—these are the musical notes of speech, out of which we fashion measures, arias, whole symphonies. There is good reason to describe beautiful speech as musical. . . . Musical

speech opens up endless possibilities of conveying the inner life of a role.[2]

Tone and rhythm give our speech color and individual flavor and make it fully human. Through careful and informed analysis of your lines, you can unlock these inherent values of tone and rhythm, and by surrendering yourself to the muscular actions required to produce them, you can bring them back to life for your audience.

EXERCISE 13.2: THE MUSIC OF SPEECH

Using the same speech you chose for your paraphrase (Exercise 13.1), analyze its rhythmic and tonal qualities. Use markings, colored pencils, or other devices to help you recognize the rhythmic and tonal patterns in the speech.

1. Using large bodily movements and nonverbal sound, create a "musical dance" of the speech that exaggerates its rhythmic and tonal patterns. Move from your deep center, and involve your breath.
2. Then immediately read the speech as written, but this time speak the words without moving. See how much of your body's memory of the first version carries over to enrich the speech as your deep muscles continue to respond to it even without external movement.
3. With your partner, examine your scene as a whole. Does the dialogue cadence give you any clues about the way the scene should flow? Together, create a musical dance of the entire scene, throwing a ball back and forth between you as the dialogue flows.

Summary of Step 13

When you set out to create a role, you necessarily begin with the character's language. You must come to "own" these words as if they were your own by re-creating and re-experiencing the living process by which that language is formed. This requires working backward from the finished language provided by the writer to discover its genesis in the mind of the character.

The words your character speaks have two kinds of meaning: their dictionary meanings, called denotation, and their emotional values, called connotation. While denotation refers to the literal meaning of words, connotation can reveal the attitudes and feelings of a character. You must consider the meanings of the words when the play was written and the feelings the words express

---

[2]From Constantin Stanislavski, *Building a Character*, trans. Elizabeth Reynolds Hapgood (New York: Theatre Arts Books, 1949), pp. 218–236. Theatre Arts Books, 153 Waverly Place, New York, NY 10014.

when used by this kind of character in this situation. One way to be sure you have examined the meanings of your lines is to paraphrase them, to restate them in your own words.

Good playwrights build in the rhythms and tonality of speech that are appropriate to a character's personality and emotion. The character's language is tied to your emotional state by the muscular activity that produces speech; an active physical participation in your character's language is a powerful tool for entering into the character's mind.

Summary of Part Three

You begin developing your character by examining the various traits specified by the writer in order to make it natural for that character to commit the actions necessary to fulfill his or her dramatic function (function traits) and also to seem like a recognizable human being (recognition traits). You consider the needs driving the character's actions and find a way to personalize those needs. Emotion recall and substitution are techniques that may assist you in doing this.

The greatest creative and personal contribution you will make to your performance is to discover the inner thought process that lies behind your character's external actions. Doing so will, in Stanislavski's terms, justify the action. In the internal process by which action is formed, a stimulus is received that generates an attitude. The stimulus may lead directly to external action without conscious choice, as an automatic action, a habit or spontaneous impulse. If an action is not automatic, a conscious thought process begins with a consideration of alternatives, called deliberation. Next, a strategic choice is made about the best way to proceed in the given circumstances. Choice is the point at which reaction turns into action, which is directed toward an objective. This action may be direct or indirect, or it may even be suppressed and thereby add to the dramatic tension. Giving words to this inner thought process is called the inner monologue. A simplified form of this process can be summed up as arousal–choice–action. You should ask yourself three questions about each of your actions: What am I reacting to? What does it make me want? What do I do to try to get it, or what *don't* I do?

Bringing the character's language to life by understanding the factors that influence that language is also crucial to the creation of your character. You examine and experience fully the word choice, rhythms, and tonalities of the language provided by the writer. Paraphrase is a good technique to ensure that you have examined each level of meaning carried by the character's language. You allow the rhythms, sounds, and breath patterns of the language to enter you fully.

PART FOUR

Final Rehearsals and Performance

The information you have gathered through analysis can make your rehearsal exploration more efficient and fruitful, but it is only a preparation for the actual work of rehearsal, not a substitute for it. The true life of your character will be found only by working with your fellow actors and director through trial and error and the accumulation of experience in rehearsal.

As you rehearse, you will put yourself into your character's world, with his or her given circumstances, and will experience them for yourself. In the character's circumstances, you will begin to experience the character's needs for yourself, perhaps recognizing similar needs from your own life. You will also begin to experience the objectives the character chooses in hopes of satisfying those needs, and these will motivate you to say and do the things the character says and does— his or her actions. As you begin to experience your character's world, needs, choices, objectives, and actions, you will find that emotion and the character's personality will begin to form in you, naturally and automatically.

This is the process that Stanislavski called transformation through the operation of the Magic If. Just as your real-life personality has been formed and continues to evolve as you interact with your world, so the character will grow during rehearsals as a new me, a new version of your I, forms under the influence of your experience of your character's circumstances, needs, objectives, actions, interactions, and relationships. As your acting skills develop, you may be able to work more efficiently and effectively, but there are no shortcuts. No amount of posturing, false voice, or trumped-up emotion can substitute for this natural process of transformation.

14

Finding the Scenario, Score, Through-Line, and Superobjective

Let's review what you learned about units of action, or beats, in Step 10. A beat may consist of several interactions between characters and is driven by a conflict produced when the objective of one character encounters the resistance or counteraction of another. Like people in everyday life, dramatic characters will pursue actions until they either succeed or fail. If their actions succeed and they achieve their objectives, they move on the next step in their pursuit of their scene objective. If they decide their actions are not working, they will try different strategies and form new actions—for example, if persuading doesn't work, they may switch to demanding. The moment at which a character changes strategy or objective signals a change in the flow of the scene as a new beat begins—that is, a beat change. We feel the rhythm of the scene as it flows from beat to beat toward the crisis, when the main conflict of the scene may be resolved or, if it is not resolved, we move on to the next step in the evolving story.

This structure is not an arbitrary choice made by the actors: It is built into the structure of the scene by the writer, although there is often room for interpretation as the actors develop their own sense of how the action flows. Every actor in a scene works to contribute to the structure of the scene, and each of them supports the beat changes when they occur, even when the particular change is not initiated by his or her character.

As you learned in Step 10, an analysis of the structure of a scene, beat by beat, is called a breakdown, or scenario. As an example of a scenario, let's look again at the scene from *A Raisin in the Sun* that we discussed earlier. Walter begins the scene with the scene objective of persuading Ruth to go to Mama with the plan for a liquor store that was suggested to him by his friend, Willy. As Ruth resists, Walter tries a number of different strategies to achieve his objective, each of which is a new action and therefore a new beat.

1. Walter begins by trying *to arouse Ruth's curiosity* about what he has been thinking about. She refuses to rise to the bait ("I know what you thinking 'bout"), and when he tells her anyway, she immediately cuts him off ("Willy Harris is a good-for-nothing loud mouth").

2. Faced with her resistance, Walter switches strategy and defends his friends, trying *to shame her* by reminding her that she cost him his chance for a successful business once before. Ruth responds by collapsing in exhaustion.

3. Walter reacts by saying that he is tired, too, and switches to the strategy of trying *to make her do her duty as a wife* because "a man needs for a woman to back him up . . ." and "Mama would listen to you." He outlines in detail how she could successfully approach Mama, ending by reminding Ruth of her place as a woman ("See there, that just goes to show you what women understand about the world").

4. The scene now reaches its crisis as Ruth counterattacks ("Walter, leave me alone!"). Walter retreats into self-pity, making one last effort *to shame her* into joining his plan by pleading that he must change his life for the sake of their son. Again she resists ("Eat your eggs, Walter").

5. Walter angrily admits defeat with an emotional outburst, and Ruth counters, "Then go to work," which carries a subtext ("Do something realistic and give up this stupid liquor store idea").

Doing a scenario in this way reveals the power struggle underlying a scene. Here, Ruth is on the defensive, and Walter initiates the beat changes until she finally counterattacks. When you add to this an understanding of Ruth's hidden pain (that she is thinking of terminating her secret pregnancy) and how much Walter's irresponsibility adds to her dilemma, you see that her short and seemingly simple responses carry a huge emotional weight.

Understanding the scenario of a scene greatly simplifies it for you. This scene, for example, can be understood as having just three beats leading to its crisis, followed by one beat of follow-through. Most importantly, notice that within each beat each character has a single objective and action. This fact permits you to translate the structure of the scene into the thoughts and actions of your character, through an understanding of how the inner action of your character contributes to the structure and flow of the scene, moment by moment.

Although doing a breakdown of a scene can inspire your rehearsal work, it is only a temporary working hypothesis, a starting point for the exploration you and your partners will make as you find the pathway of action that the author has hidden beneath the surface of the dialogue and as the living rhythm of the scene begins to emerge. Most accomplished actors have internalized this sense of scene structure and rhythm and approach it intuitively, in the same way that an accomplished musician applies the old adage "Play the music, not the notes."

THE SCORE AND PACE

As your exploration of the scene develops in rehearsal, you will begin to feel the logical flow of the sequence of your character's objectives. As he or she pursues an objective through a strategic action, a point will be reached when the strategy either fails or succeeds. If it fails, your character will switch to a new strategy; if it succeeds, he or she will move on to their next objective. There will be some reason that makes each change seem like a good choice under the circumstances, and this gives the sequence a unity and coherence. Stanislavski called this sequence of objectives the **score** of the role; discovering and experiencing the logic of this sequence can carry you through the scene with a natural momentum. As Stanislavski said:

> With time and frequent repetition, in rehearsal and performance, this score becomes habitual. An actor becomes so accustomed to all his objectives and their sequence that he cannot conceive of approaching his role otherwise than along the line of the steps fixed in the score. . . . The score automatically stirs the actor to physical action.[1]

This sense of the underlying score of the scene will help you in many ways. For one, it will make it easier to learn your lines. One of my actor friends says that he likes to "learn the action" before he "learns the words."

Most importantly, a good sense of scene structure becomes a shared "map" that permits the actors to support one another in their journey through the scene. The map helps to lessen your fear of becoming lost, making your work more playful and creative. It also helps you to experience the scene as a single, rhythmic event.

One symptom that the scene has started to "play" well is that it will take less effort on your part; the scene will seem to run under its own power. It will also begin to seem shorter to you. Sometimes, when a scene really plays well for the first time, you may feel as if you must have skipped something; you may find that you can't remember what happened very well. This occurs because you were more moved than moving—that is, the scene was "doing you" instead of the other way around.

It is this natural flow of action that we call good **pace**. Pace is the momentum with which the scene flows, regardless of its tempo; a fast farce scene and a slow scene from a classical tragedy can each have good pace if the connections that move us from one beat to another are strong and fully realized. Sometimes the best thing to do, if the pace of a scene is falling and the event is feeling lifeless and artificial, is to slow down temporarily. This allows you and your partners to fully experience each transaction and the connections that move the scene from interaction to interaction, and from beat to beat.

---

[1]Constantin Stanislavski, *Creating a Role,* trans. Elizabeth Reynolds Hapgood (New York: Theatre Arts Books, 1961), p. 62.

THE THROUGH-LINE AND SUPEROBJECTIVE

You learned in Part 2 that a good story is structured on several levels of action: Individual interactions make up beats, beats make up scenes, and scenes form the overall shape of the rising and falling action of the entire story, giving unity to the whole. These levels of action relate directly to the inner life of your character; you will have an objective on each level. In each beat you will have a beat objective; the beat objectives will lead toward your scene objective; and your scene objective can be seen as springing from a deep, overall objective that is your character's **superobjective**.

The idea of a superobjective is easier to grasp if you think of it as a life goal or a guiding principle governing your character's behavior, often on an unconscious level. Think of someone you know well, and see if there seems to be a life goal at work in him or her. Such drives are basic, like the desire for love, respect, security, or aliveness. They can also be "negatives," such as the avoidance of failure or ridicule. And they can be idealistic, such as a passion for justice or freedom. It is not often easy to identify someone's superobjective, unless you have a lot of experience with the person and know him or her well. In a similar way, your understanding of your character's superobjective will develop gradually as you rehearse; it will be the *result* of your experience of the role, not a prerequisite for it. Nonetheless, it may be useful to form a general idea of the superobjective early on, knowing that your understanding may change as your work progresses.

For example, consider again the scene we have already discussed from *Death of a Salesman*. When Willy finds Howard engrossed in his new recorder, Willy's beat objective is to get Howard's attention so he can move toward his scene objective of getting an assignment in town. This scene objective is connected directly to Willy's superobjective, to be a successful salesman, which for Willy is a way *to prove himself a worthy human being by earning money and respect*. (Notice that defining the superobjective, just as defining objectives on any level, requires using a transitive verb.) You might even find a line from the play that sums it up; for example, Willy says, "Be liked and you will never want."

If we follow each of Willy's beat and scene objectives throughout the play, we see in each case how he is led from objective to objective in pursuit of his superobjective. The logic of this sequence of objectives striving toward the superobjective is called the **through-line** of the role. Stanislavski described it like this:

> In a play the whole stream of individual minor objectives, all the imaginative thoughts, feelings and actions of an actor should converge to carry out this superobjective. . . . Also this impetus toward the superobjective must be continuous throughout the whole play.[2]

---

[2]Constantin Stanislavski, *An Actor's Handbook,* trans. and ed. Elizabeth Reynolds Hapgood (New York: Theatre Arts Books, 1936), p 56. Copyright © 1936, 1961, 1963 by Elizabeth Reynolds Hapgood.

Stanislavski once said that each of a character's actions fits into the through-line like vertebrae in a spine. Therefore, some actors call the through-line the **spine** of the role.

Identifying your character's through-line of action as being driven by his or her superobjective can help you to better understand each of your specific objectives, connecting each to the character's deepest needs and desires. It can also help you to see that the sequence of objectives has a single driving force; thus, you can **play through** each moment and achieve both unity and momentum (good pace) in your performance.

Your character's superobjective may be conscious or (more commonly) unconscious. If the character is not conscious of it, you—the actor—will have to treat it in a special way. You should take it fully into account as you work, but you should not let your knowledge of it as an actor "contaminate" your character's reality. Remember the idea of dual consciousness: What you know as an actor is not the same as what your character knows. The acting teacher Lee Strasberg once said the hardest thing about acting is "not knowing what you know."

In some cases, a character with an unconscious superobjective may become conscious of it at some point. Such moments of self-insight are major events and may indeed be the point of an entire story, as when Shakespeare's King Lear finally says to the daughter he has wronged, "Pray you now, forget and forgive; I am old and foolish."

Whether or not your character is conscious of his or her superobjective, it functions as an underlying principle that affects all of your actions and establishes your attitude toward life. Willy Loman tries to earn self-esteem through selling; he confuses success as a salesman with success as a human being. Each moment, each beat, each scene, and every aspect of Willy's psychology can be understood as reflecting his superobjective. Eventually, he is no longer able to sell either his products or himself, and his last "sale" becomes his suicide, making the insurance money his last "paycheck." Thus, this final, desperate act (which is the climax of the play) is the fulfillment of Willy's tragically misguided way of pursuing his superobjective. By experiencing how each moment, beat, and scene of your character's behavior is driven by his or her superobjective, you will fulfill what Stanislavski called the actor's main task: to understand how every moment of the performance contributes to the reason the play was written.

EXERCISE 14.1: IDENTIFYING THE SUPEROBJECTIVE

1. Taking the entire play into account, describe your character's superobjective, using a transitive verb phrase such as "to be thought of as a worthy human being."
2. Specify the kind of strategies your character commonly uses to try to achieve this superobjective, such as "to be thought of as a worthy human being by making sales and earning the smiles of my clients."
3. Is your character conscious or unconscious of this life goal? Is there a moment when he or she becomes conscious of it?

PERSONALIZING THE SUPEROBJECTIVE

Because the superobjective of most major characters is fairly universal, it is usually not difficult to personalize. Like Willy Loman, we all want to be thought of as worthy, and thus we can all identify with Willy, however much we can see that Willy's way of pursuing self-esteem is mistaken. You must make the most of any connections you find between your character's goals and your own.

There may be characters, however, whose life goals are difficult for you to find in yourself. In these cases, you may be able to substitute some analogous need of your own, or you may simply need to use your imaginative skill to create the superobjective in yourself. However you do it, you need to base your work on this kind of deeply personal and real experience of the character's deepest needs and energies.

It may be more difficult to describe the superobjective of minor characters, because the writer has not provided much information about them. Here you can be inventive, so long as your understanding of the character enables you to accurately serve his or her dramatic function within the play as a whole.

The superobjective naturally colors the way a character sees him- or herself. Willy's superobjective, for example, is to prove himself worthy by earning money and respect, so his underlying self-image must be that he is *un*worthy as a human being, and much of his behavior seems perversely dedicated to proving his own unworthiness. Because self-image is often a self-fulfilling prophecy, you may be able to discover your character's superobjectve by examining his or her attitude toward him- or herself.

EXERCISE 14.2: SELF-IMAGE

1. What is your character's dominant self-image? Enter into your character's frame of mind, and complete these phrases:
   a. The most beautiful part of my body is . . .
   b. Happiness to me is . . .
   c. The thing I most want to do before I die is . . .
   d. The ugliest part of my body is . . .
   e. The thing I like best about myself is . . .
   f. Pain to me is . . .
   g. My mother . . .
   h. The most secret thing about me is . . .
   i. I can hear my father's voice speaking through my own when I tell myself . . .
   j. Love to me is . . .
   k. If you could hear the music in me . . .
   l. I want my epitaph to be . . .
2. Now, immediately work through the scene, and allow these feelings to affect you.

Again, avoid the temptation to indicate. It is never your aim to explain your superobjective to the audience; your job is to create experience, not to explain behavior.

EXERCISE 14.3: PERSONALIZING THE SUPEROBJECTIVE

1. Can you identify some deep need of your own, some life goal, which is similar to that of the character? If not, do you have some deep desire that is analogous to the character's or that you can substitute for the character's?
2. Discuss with your partner how both of your superobjectives are expressed in the scene. Do they relate to one another in a way that enhances the drama of the scene?
3. Perform the scene for your group. Did you feel the superobjective driving you? Was the through-line strong? Did the score give the scene good pace? Did you avoid indicating?

Summary of Step 14

The flow of the sequence of your character's objectives is called the score of the role; it can help you to play through each moment and achieve both unity and momentum, giving the performance good pace regardless of its tempo.

Your character has objectives on three levels: Immediate beat objectives are derived from the scene objectives, and scene objectives spring from a deep, overall objective that is your character's life goal, or superobjective. The logic of the sequence of objectives is the score of the role, and this sequence is driven by the character's superobjective. Striving toward the superobjective is called the through-line (or spine) of the role. Ideally, the sense of the superobjective will emerge gradually from your experience of your character's specific actions; it is a result of your rehearsal exploration, not a substitute for it, and must be felt by you on a deeply personal level.

15 Staging

As you prepare your scene for final performance, you must begin to consider what adjustments may be needed to make your work accessible to an audience. Your first consideration will be the physical and vocal adjustments that may be required by the stage on which you will perform.

TYPES OF STAGES

A stage is defined by its spatial relationship to the audience. There are four basic types of stage configurations: proscenium, thrust, arena, and environmental (see Figure 15.1). Let's consider what each of the basic types means to an actor.

Proscenium

The traditional proscenium stage features an arch through which the audience sees the action. This "picture frame" evolved as a way of establishing a point of reference for settings painted in perspective (hence, the word *proscenium*, which means "in front of the scene"). An actor on a proscenium stage must, of course, realize that the audience is limited to one side of the playing area. In realistic plays, the walls of the set and the placement of furniture are splayed open to audience view, creating a somewhat artificial environment. It will be your job to play within this artificial space so as to create the entire environment, including the invisible "fourth wall" that separates audience and stage. Some directors and actors think that, like the set and furniture, actors must also **cheat out** (turn their bodies partly out toward the audience), but this is not as necessary as some think. Cheating out makes characters look as if they are

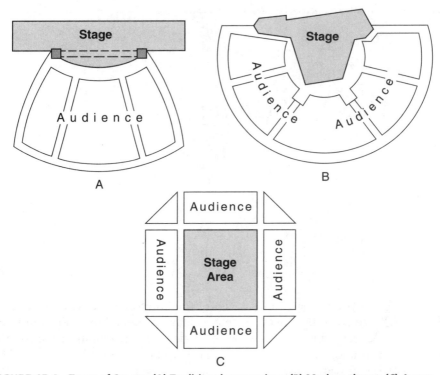

FIGURE 15.1 Types of Stages: (A) Traditional proscenium; (B) Modern thrust; (C) Arena.

more interested in speaking to the audience than to the other characters in the scene. So although you may make some adjustments because of the audience's location, you must do so without destroying the logic of the character's relationships. Don't underestimate how much acting you can do with your back.

Depending on the size of the house, the proscenium (and the other types of stages as well) may require an adjustment in the overall **scale** of the performance. In order to be heard and seen well, you may have to speak louder and move bigger. In a very large house, it may even be necessary to deliver your lines toward the audience; this is especially true in many outdoor theaters, such as those in which most summer Shakespeare festivals occur.

Thrust

The thrust stage (so called because it "thrusts" into the midst of the audience) features the same stage/audience relationship as that found in classical and Elizabethan theaters; it places an actor in proximity to the audience but also limits the use of scenery. For this reason, it is very much an actor's theater. For the actor, there is some added responsibility to stay open to audience view or at least to distribute his or her presence equally to all sections of the house.

The thrust stage has not just one but three invisible walls; there is usually scenery at the rear and furniture or objects arranged throughout the stage, and you will have to play the full reality of the environment. It is important on a thrust stage for the actors to stand further apart than usual; if they are too close, they will block one another from audience view and will throw shadows on one another's faces. The increased sense of audience contact inherent in the thrust stage requires a detailed and subtle performance.

Arena

The arena and other types of full-round or three-quarter round stages stand at the opposite extreme from proscenium stages. Here the audience surrounds the stage, and all four walls are invisible, though doorways and windows are sometimes indicated by physical elements. The arena stage offers the greatest sense of intimacy of all stage types and is usually relatively small. Audiences tend to expect an even more detailed and subtle performance here than in other kinds of theaters, something closer to what is required for film acting. The completeness of the performance helps to compensate for the fact that an actor's back is always to some part of the audience.

Environmental

Although most stages are of the three basic types just described, we sometimes create special environments for specific productions, some of which may entirely eliminate the separation of stage and audience. Here, of course, the proximity of the audience demands total commitment and attention to detail, just as the camera does in film acting.[1]

Whatever adjustment in scale is required by the space in which you will perform, you must justify it by also adjusting the level of energy driving your inner process so that the larger actions are believable and natural within the space. Trust that the audience will willingly join with you in accepting the adjustments required by the conditions of performance.

> ### EXERCISE 15.1: JUSTIFYING ADJUSTMENTS IN SCALE
>
> Select a section from your scene for this experiment in making an adjustment in scale. Justify each of the following adjustments that might be demanded by the theater space in which you perform:
>
> **1.** Do the scene as if for a huge proscenium auditorium.
> **2.** Do the scene as if for a moderate-sized thrust stage.
> **3.** Do the scene as if for a small arena stage or a film.

MOVING ON STAGE

When we discuss movement and position on stage, we use a standard nomenclature that you must learn. Movements toward or away from the audience are described by very old terms, which were developed for the proscenium stage at

---

[1]The demands of film acting are described in detail in Robert Benedetti, *ACTION! Acting for Film and Television* (Boston: Allyn & Bacon, 2001).

a time when the stage floor was sloped upward away from the audience in order to enhance the illusion of perspective. Even today, moving away from the audience is called going **upstage**, and moving toward the audience is going **downstage**. To stand "level" with another actor is for both of you to stand at the same distance from the audience. (Moving upstage during a scene so that the other actors are forced to turn their backs on the audience in order to speak to you is called **upstaging**; avoid it.)

Lateral directions are determined by the actors' view as they face the audience. Thus, **stage right** is the same as the audience's left; "downstage right" means toward the audience and to the actor's right (see Figure 15.2).

Turns are described as being either **in** (toward the center of the stage, from whichever side of the stage you are on) or **out** (away from the center). **Crossing** (that is, moving from one point to another) may be in a straight line, or in a slight arc so that you end facing more in profile to the audience. A cross with an exaggerated arc is called a "circle cross" (or sometimes a "banana").

Positions as you pivot relative to the audience are called "one-quarter," "half," and "three-quarters," depending on how far you turn from one side to the other. Thus, a director may tell you to "cheat out one-quarter," which means to pivot 45 degrees away from center. This system of directions can soon become second nature to you.

EXERCISE 15.2: DIRECTIONS ON STAGE

Have your partner stand in the center of the stage, with you standing beside him or her on the stage right side. Let your partner "play director" first by giving you the following directions. When you have finished, switch places.

Go down right. / Turn out and go up right. / Take a long cross down left, going upstage of me. / Turn in and do a circle cross up,

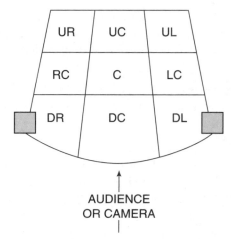

FIGURE 15.2 Locations on Proscenium Stage.

passing on the downstage side of me and ending level with me on the right. / Cheat out one-quarter. / Circle up to the right around me, and exit left center.

BLOCKING

Blocking is the way in which the actors move in relation to one another and within the space determined by the design of the set. The spatial configuration of the set and the placement of entranceways and furniture or other objects are called the *groundplan*. Because you don't have a director or designer to provide a groundplan for your scene, you and your partner will have to determine it for yourselves. Keep it simple, with the minimum of furniture or props required by the action.

Good blocking always springs from the relationship of the characters and the underlying action of the scene. Blocking at its best expresses things such as Who is dominant at this moment in the scene? What space does this person control? Who is on whose side? Who is on the attack? Who is retreating? Is there a counterattack? Blocking is just dead movement and positioning until it has been justified by inner action, much like any other external element of the performance.

Although the sense of spatial relationship is artistically heightened on the stage, it is based on the way people relate to one another spatially in everyday life. Look around you and observe how the locations people take in a room reflect their relationships and attitudes. Notice how changes in relationship are reflected by the movements people make, as they move closer or further away from one another or change position within the space they share. These are the kinds of impulses you will feel as you experience your action on stage—they are the basis of your blocking. Let yourself move!

You have probably already found the basics of the blocking for your scene during your earlier rehearsals as you felt the impulse to move in relationship to your partner. Build on what you have already discovered, edit it for clarity and accessibility to the audience, but do not embellish or add movement just for its own sake. For now, don't be overly concerned with onlookers; play directly to one another as if you were on an arena stage, and don't falsify your relationship by cheating out toward the audience.

EXERCISE 15.3: BLOCKING

1. Spend a few days watching the "blocking" of everyday life; notice how attitude, relationship, and action are expressed in the way people place themselves in a room and move in relationship to each other. Make notes in your journal.
2. After creating a simple groundplan, work with your partner to block your scene; make the blocking an effective expression of the relationship and action in the scene. Follow your impulses.

When you are working with a director, he or she may have various approaches to blocking. Some directors preplan the blocking in detail, but most prefer that the actors provide the impulses that generate the blocking, which the director will then edit as needed. Regardless of what method your director uses, your main responsibility is to justify your stage movement so that it grows out of an inner need and expresses your relationship with the other characters in the scene. If your director requests a piece of blocking that feels awkward, you may have to supply the justification in your own mind. (Remember that in most theaters, the director is the final authority on *what* and the actor is the final authority on *how*.) Sometimes a director may be using the blocking to tell you something about the action. If he or she asks you to "move into her," the director may really be saying, "This is where you counterattack."

SHAPING AND PACING

Now that you are well into the rehearsal of your scene, you and your partner are beginning to shape and specify the instances of action–reaction that form the flow that binds the scene together. As you feel the connectedness of every moment with every other moment, your through-line begins to emerge, and the scene begins "to play," to flow under its own power. You no longer have to *make* things happen; you can *let* them happen. As a result, your scene begins to feel simpler and shorter. Finding and perfecting these connections is the most important business of your final rehearsals.

> **EXERCISE 15.4: MAKING CONNECTIONS**
>
> Work through your scene with your partner, allowing either of you to stop the rehearsal at any point when you do not feel connected to the flow of the action, when your partner is not "making" you do what you must do next.
>
> At each point of difficulty, examine the moments that led up to it; what does either of you need from the other to induce the next action? Work together so that every moment of the scene grows organically out of the flow of action and reaction.
>
> **Note:** Do not tell your partner what to do; instead, ask for what you *need*, and leave it to your partner to provide it. You might, for example, say something like "I need to be more threatened by that" but leave it to your partner to determine how best to threaten you.

In this late stage of rehearsal, each beat change and the scene crisis are brought into sharp focus. Accordingly, the flow of action that connects these elements is established and smoothed to provide a sense of urgency, significance, rising dramatic tension, and the momentum that is good pace. One important element of good pace is **cueing**, the way one character begins to speak after another has finished. In real life, if you and I are discussing something, I listen to you in order to understand the idea you are trying to express. When I have grasped the idea, I form my response and am usually ready to begin answering before you have actually finished your sentence. Listen to real-life conversations; do you hear how we sometimes overlap one another's speeches slightly or at least are ready to respond before the other person has stopped talking? This is good cueing.

EXERCISE 15.5: SHAPING AND PACING THE SCENE (DRESS REHEARSAL)

1. Provide any simple furniture or props you need, and dress appropriately for this final rehearsal.
2. Together, find the aspects of the situation that provide the urgency or sense of deadline that will drive the scene's momentum:
   a. The physical environment: time, place, and so on
   b. The social environment: customs, the presence of others
   c. The situation: internal or external factors that create urgency or tension
   d. The conflict between you
3. Practice your listening and responding skills to produce good cueing.

Summary of Step 15

In the final phase of work you will consider what adjustments are necessary to make your performance accessible to your audience. Your first consideration is the type of stage on which you will perform: Proscenium, thrust, arena, and environmental stages each make special demands. Also, the size of the house will determine adjustments in the scale of your performance. In this final stage of rehearsal, your scene will begin to play under its own power, feeling simpler and shorter, and will be adjusted to meet the demands of your performance space. You now develop the blocking, which is the way the characters move within the configuration of the groundplan. Good blocking always springs from the relationships of the characters and the underlying action of the scene. You shape and pace the scene by clarifying its structure and practicing good cueing.

16 Performing

Having laid the foundation of your score and characterization, having set the basic form of the blocking, and having established good shape and pace, your scene is almost ready to be performed. If you were working in a fully mounted production instead of a classroom situation, this final phase of the rehearsal process would be devoted to incorporating the physical production elements: makeup, props, costumes, set, lights, and sound. Ideally, this would be a time of completion and crystallization of your performance; many actors do not feel that their work comes fully to life until all the physical production elements are in place. Stanislavski himself spoke of completing a characterization only when, in full makeup and costume, he would rehearse before a mirror to be sure that his external appearance was correct.

In most American theaters, the final week or so of rehearsal is devoted to the assimilation of all the completed technical elements and is called *tech and dress*. This can be a period of tremendous frustration and distraction for actors if they have not prepared for it in the earlier stages of rehearsal. Above all, actors must avoid the temptation to "freeze" the work during this final phase of rehearsal. Many fine performances wither on the vine before opening because the outer form becomes the focus of the actors' attention and the inner phase of action ceases to live and grow. Instead, actors should use the addition of the technical elements as an opportunity to extend and specify the scores of their roles and to explore further the lives of their characters within a more complete environment.

There are two main ways in which you can be prepared for this final phase: first, by having a solid score (the sequence of objectives), which helps you to keep your focus on the action without being distracted by all the new elements; and second, by having previously used good rehearsal substitutes for props, costumes, furniture, and groundplan.

During this final period, you will probably have less rehearsal time available to you as the energies of the production are taken up with technical matters. It is important that you continue to work on your own to prepare yourself for the coming of the audience. One way to do this is to *visualize* the performance as it would be under audience conditions, and this you can do even in your classroom situation. Visualization is an excellent form of private rehearsal; it is most effective when used during periods of relaxation, when your deep muscles will actually participate. Here is an exercise in the technique called **visuo-motor behavior rehearsal (VMBR)**, which was first developed for the 1980 Winter Olympics and is used today with great effectiveness by many athletes.

EXERCISE 16.1: VISUO-MOTOR BEHAVIOR REHEARSAL

1. Using the Phasic Relaxation exercise (3.2), put yourself into deep muscle relaxation and restful alertness.
2. Now visualize the night when you are about to open in the play from which your scene comes; the theater is ready, you hear the buzz of the audience in the house, and you are standing in your costume with your fellow actors, ready to take your places.
3. In your mind, go into the set, and take your opening position; feel the stage lights shining on you, smell the makeup, feel your clothing, see your fellow actors and the set.
4. Let the scene begin; live through it totally, and let your deep muscles respond actively to the experience.

Tests have shown that this form of rehearsal can be just as effective as an ordinary rehearsal, and sometimes more so.

EMOTION IN PERFORMANCE

Young actors sometimes think they must re-create the character's emotion in order to generate each performance "truthfully," but this is an exhausting and unreliable way of working. Since emotion arises from action, you need only *do* what your character does and *think* the thoughts involved in the action; the performance itself will then give you the emotion.

We may sometimes be tempted to admire the emotionality of an actor who loses control and is overwhelmed, but a display of emotion for its own sake is never our true purpose. A great actor aspires to use emotional technique to realize the truth of a character according to the demands of the material. Stanislavski said it this way:

> Our art . . . requires that an actor experience the agony of his role, and weep his heart out at home or in rehearsals, that he then calm himself, get rid of every sentiment alien or obstructive to his part. He then comes out on the stage to convey to the audience in clear, pregnant, deeply felt, intelligible and eloquent terms what he has been through. At this point the spectators will be more affected than

the actor, and he will conserve all his forces in order to direct them where he needs them most of all—in reproducing the inner life of the character he is portraying.[1]

The important idea here is that in performance "the spectators will be more affected than the actor." This is necessary for several reasons. First, strong emotion will interfere with an actor's craftsmanship; as Stanislavski put it, "A person in the midst of experiencing a poignant emotional drama is incapable of speaking of it coherently."[2] Second, emotions are unreliable in generating a performance that must be done repeatedly and on schedule. Stanislavski used the example of an opera singer who, at the moment the music requires a certain note with a certain feeling, cannot say to the conductor, "I'm not feeling it yet, give me four more measures."

SPONTANEITY

What you do in performance should feel spontaneous, as if for the first time, no matter how many times you have done it before. To achieve this spontaneity, you must keep your awareness on your objective, rather than on the mechanics of your external action—just as a baseball batter must think only about the ball and not about his swing. Otherwise you will only be going through the motions, repeating the external aspects of your performance without re-experiencing the internal needs that drive the externals.

Notice that spontaneity does not mean that your performance is erratic or changeable: During the rehearsal process, you gradually refine your external action until it becomes dependable, consistent, stageworthy, and automatic— just as the baseball batter has rehearsed all the aspects of his swing until he can do it without thinking. As Stanislavski said,

> A spontaneous action is one that, through frequent repetition in rehearsal and performance, has become automatic and therefore free.[3]

Because you are able to perform your action without thinking about it, your mind is free to concentrate fully on your objective and to experience your action as if for the first time and in the here and now.

EXERCISE 16.2: FINAL PERFORMANCE

Using substitute furniture, props, and costumes, prepare as complete a final performance of your scene as you are able. If you are in a

---

[1]Constantin Stanislavski, *Building a Character*, trans. Elizabeth Reynolds Hapgood (New York: Theatre Arts Books, 1949), p. 70. Theatre Arts Books, 153 Waverly Place, New York, NY 10014.
[2]Constantin Stanislavski, *Building a Character*, trans. Elizabeth Reynolds Hapgood (New York: Theatre Arts Books, 1949), p. 70. Theatre Arts Books, 153 Waverly Place, New York, NY 10014.
[3]Constantin Stanislavski, *An Actor's Handbook*, trans. and ed. Elizabeth Reynolds Hapgood (New York: Theatre Arts Books, 1936), p. 138. Copyright © 1936, 1961, 1963 by Elizabeth Reynolds Hapgood.

class situation, consider presenting a program of all the group's final scenes for an invited audience. Allow yourself to be spontaneous, and let emotion arise of its own accord. Experience something of the thrill of an opening night.

EVALUATING YOUR WORK

The fundamental drives for most actors, like most people, are the desire for success and, its flip side, the fear of failure. The desire for success can give you tremendous energy and the courage to take risks, while the fear of failure encourages safe and conservative choices, leading, at best, to technical skill that can never entirely compensate for a lack of creativity.

An excessive fear of failure can cause you to censor creative impulses, fearing that you'll look foolish, and encourages you to continually judge your own performance to see whether you are doing it right. This produces self-consciousness and tension. Although a small part of every actor's consciousness is necessarily reserved for ongoing artistic evaluation of a performance, this awareness must only *witness*, not *control*, the performance.

The desire for success carries its own dangers. There are two ways of measuring success: in *internal* terms—such as pride, sense of accomplishment, and feelings of growth—and by *external* measurements—such as reviews, grades, and the response of an audience. Obviously, all actors are concerned with both types; what is needed is perspective and balance between the two.

Most actors err on the side of emphasizing external measures of success over internal. Even if they have a sense of their own work, actors usually don't trust it, and they feel so dependent on the opinions of others that a negative response from anyone damages their self-esteem. Although it hurts any actor when his or her work is not received well, a serious actor strives to balance the desire for immediate success with the equally important long-range need for artistic development. You should approach each new role, each rehearsal, and each performance with a desire not only to please others, but also to satisfy your own needs, to learn and grow for yourself. When evaluating your experience, you must ask not only, "Did I do the job well?" but also, "Am I now a better human being and a better actor for having done it?"

EXERCISE 16.3: MEASURING SUCCESS

Think back to your performance. Given that all actors have anxiety about performing, did your anxiety stay within controllable limits? Did you experience destructive tension? Did you censor yourself? Did you manage to stay in the moment?

Did you have your own independent evaluation of your performance? Did you trust that evaluation? How did the comments of others affect you? Did you distinguish between the short-term measurement of your success in the role and the long-term benefits of the work for you as a developing artist? Did the experience satisfy some personal need and thereby help you to grow as a human being?

GROWTH AFTER OPENING

In the live theater, the opening of a show is never the completion of an actor's work, but only the start of a new phase of the growth process. The audience contributes in many ways, perhaps most by providing the responses that complete the rhythmic shaping of the work. These responses take many forms, from the overt (such as laughter or sobs) to the covert (such as rapt stillness or restlessness, or just the "feeling" inside the auditorium). Whatever their form, the audience's responses are an important element in the rhythm of a scene. So far, you have been guessing what those responses would be—and if you had a director, he or she would have been substituting for them as an ideal audience of one—but now you have the real thing, and you can fine-tune the shape and flow of your action accordingly. This is the business of preview performances or invited audiences at dress rehearsals, if you are lucky enough to have them.

The audience's presence will also cause a change in the way you experience your own work; some things you thought would work well may turn out to be too personal or obscure, while other things that you hadn't really noticed may turn out to be powerful or worth developing further. At last you have a sure basis for judgment.

This sure basis will naturally cause you to begin economizing. You will find after a time that you expended more energy during rehearsals than you do in performance and that you will generally expend less and less energy as the run continues. This is not because you begin doing your part mechanically, without thought or feeling, but because you are penetrating deeper and deeper to its essence; as this happens, nonessential detail begins to fall away. Your performance is made more effective by distilling it to its essentials in this way; you are doing more with less.

AN ACTOR'S SENSE OF PURPOSE

As an actor, your sense of purpose grows from your respect for your own talent, your love for the specific material you are performing, and your desire to use both to serve your audience. This drive to be of service through your art will finally overcome the self-consciousness of your ego and carry you beyond yourself, giving you a transcendent purpose from which will come courage, dignity, fulfillment, and ongoing artistic vitality.

Stanislavsky called this ongoing artistic vitality "theatrical youthfulness." Near the end of his life, he addressed a group of young actors who were entering the Moscow Art Theatre with these words:

> The first essential to retain a youthful performance is to keep the idea of the play alive. That is why the dramatist wrote it and that is why you decided to produce it. One should not be on the stage, one should not put on a play for the sake of acting or producing only. Yes, you must be excited about your profession. You must love it devotedly and passionately, but not for itself, not for its laurels, not for

the pleasure and delight it brings to you as artists. You must love your chosen profession because it gives you the opportunity to communicate ideas that are important and necessary to your audience. Because it gives you the opportunity, through the ideas that you dramatize on the stage and through your characterizations, to educate your audience and to make them better, finer, wiser, and more useful members of society. . . . You must keep the idea alive and be inspired by it at each performance. This is the only way to retain youthfulness in performance and your own youthfulness as actors. The true recreation of the play's idea—I emphasize the word true—demands from the artist wide and varied knowledge, constant self-discipline, the subordination of his personal tastes and habits to the demands of the idea, and sometimes even definite sacrifices.[4]

The art of acting has always had a very special service to render, one that has become increasingly important today. An actor's ability to transform, to become someone else, to be in charge of personal reality, can be a source of hope and inspiration to others. The actor's ability to redefine personal reality before our very eyes reminds us of our own spiritual capacity for self-definition, and thus the theater becomes a celebration of our vitality and of the ongoing flow of life. Although a play may teach us something about who we are, it is an actor's ability to be transformed that teaches us something about who we may *become*. An actor who works in this spirit finds his or her horizons being continually broadened by a renewed sense of ethical and spiritual purpose. It can be a wonderful time to be an actor.

Summary of Step 16

When your scene is nearly ready to perform, in a fully mounted production you would add the final technical elements. Technical and dress rehearsals can be a period of tremendous distraction for the actor who has not prepared properly with a strong score and effective use of the rehearsal furniture, groundplan, props, and costume pieces. You should strive to keep each performance fresh and spontaneous without making it erratic. Your emotional experience should be controlled and should not become an end in itself. You should evaluate your work not only in terms of the response of others, but also in terms of your own long-term growth objectives. The opening of a show is never the completion of your work, but only the start of a new phase of the growth process. At last you will have a sure basis for judgment, and you will penetrate deeper and deeper to the essence of your role; as this happens, nonessential detail begins to fall away. Your performance is made more effective by distilling it to its essentials; you will be doing more with less. As an actor, your sense of purpose will give you courage and ongoing artistic vitality.

---

[4]Nikolai Gorchakov, *Stanislavski Directs* (New York: Funk & Wagnalls, 1954), pp. 40-41.

Summary of Part Four

The most important discoveries are made during the actual rehearsal process as you explore your role with your fellow actors under the guidance of your director. In this day-by-day work, you begin to experience the action in specific relationships and find personal significance in your character's needs, choices, objectives, and actions. As you begin to re-create the inner process by which re-action becomes action, either automatically or through deliberation and choice, interaction by interaction, you begin to transform as a new me emerges, a new version of yourself. Thus, your character is formed by the same process that forms your everyday personality, by your experience of actually living as if you were in the character's world, feeling the character's needs as if they were your own, making the choices he or she would make as if they were your own, and doing the things the character would do to try to achieve his or her objectives in each beat and each scene and overall as he or she strives toward a superobjective. This sequence of objectives emerges as your map of the role, the score that will guide and inspire you through the entire performance with good pace and economy.

In the final stages of rehearsal, you shape your performance to be stageworthy and dependable. You adapt it to your stage space and develop blocking that expresses the action and relationships. You perform it with controlled spontaneity and emotional clarity so as to fulfill the dramatic function of the role. You evaluate your work by balancing your own judgment with that of others, considering always your growth as an actor, your commitment to the material, and your sense of purpose in the world you serve through your work.

As an actor, your sense of purpose grows from your respect for your own talent, your love for the specific material you are performing, and your desire to use both to serve your audience. This drive to be of service through your art will finally overcome the self-consciousness of your ego and carry you beyond yourself, giving you a transcendent purpose from which will come courage, dignity, fulfillment, and ongoing artistic vitality.

APPENDIX A
A SAMPLE TELEVISION SCENE

FROM *CHEERS* BY TOM REEDER[24]

[Carla works as a waitress in the Cheers bar, which is managed by Diane. In this scene, Carla has just received an offer of marriage from Ben Ludlow, an eminent psychologist she has been dating. She has reacted strangely to the proposal and has gone into the back room to think. Diane follows her to see what's wrong.]

[Interior pool room. Carla is standing lost in thought. Diane enters.]

DIANE: Carla, I couldn't help noticing that you're not exactly leaping for joy. Bennett Ludlow is a wonderful catch.

CARLA *[WITH DIFFICULTY]*: There are things he doesn't know about me.

DIANE: A little mystery is good for a marriage. What haven't you told him?

CARLA: Well, I haven't been completely honest about my kids.

DIANE: What haven't you told him about them?

CARLA: That they live.

DIANE: He doesn't know you have children?

CARLA: Shhhhh!

DIANE: Carla, you have to tell him. He's going to wonder who those little people are running around the house.

CARLA: I'm hoping he'll be too polite to ask.

[Off Diane's look.]

CARLA *(CONT'D)*: I didn't want to scare him off.

DIANE: Seriously, Carla, it's only fair that you tell him immediately that you have five children.

CARLA: Six.

DIANE: Okay, six. But if you wait, if you put this off—I thought it was five?

CARLA: It was. But I just came from the doctor.

[Diane groans with recognition.]

DIANE: Carla, when you took hygiene in high school, did you cut the "how-not-to" lecture?

CARLA: I had to. I was pregnant. I tell you I'm the most fertile woman who ever lived. For me there's only one method of birth control that's absolutely foolproof, but it makes me sick to my stomach.

DIANE: What's that?

CARLA: Saying no.

[Ludlow enters.]

LUDLOW: Carla, are you all right?

DIANE: Well, I'm going to go celebrate with the others. We're like a big family here at Cheers. You know what they say about a big family— more to love. I always say—

CARLA: Beat it.

DIANE: Bye.

[Diane exits.]

LUDLOW: Carla, my proposal wasn't received with the enthusiasm I ex- pected it to be. In fact, it occurred to me that I never actually heard you say "yes."

CARLA: I know. Benny, I have to tell you some things about myself.

LUDLOW: This sounds serious.

CARLA: It is. Benny, have you ever seen "The Brady Bunch"?

LUDLOW: Yes, I think so.

CARLA: Picture them with knives.

LUDLOW: I don't understand.

CARLA: I have five children.

LUDLOW: Five?

CARLA: Well . . . five and counting. You're going to be a daddy.

[Ludlow sits down.]

LUDLOW: This is quite a day.

CARLA: You now have my permission to withdraw the proposal.

LUDLOW: Do you want me to withdraw the proposal, Carla?

CARLA: I want you to do what you want to do.

LUDLOW: I want to marry you.

CARLA: You're kidding. Wow. What class.

LUDLOW: I still haven't heard you say yes.

CARLA: I know. *[Genuinely puzzled]* Why do you think that is?

LUDLOW: I think if you examine your feelings, you'll know.

CARLA: Yeah, I guess I know. I love somebody else.

LUDLOW: Who?

CARLA: I don't know his name. I haven't met him yet, but I've had this real clear picture of him in my mind for what seems like forever. He's going to walk into this bar some night. Actually, not walk. More like swagger. You know, confident but not cocky. He's okay-looking, but he's no pretty boy. He's a swell dresser. He's wearing this burgundy leather jacket. His nose is broken in all the right places. He's got this scar on his chin he won't talk about. He cracks his knuckles all the time. Drives me up the wall, but, what can you do? Doesn't talk much. Doesn't have to. He falls for me hard. I hurt him a few times. He gets over it. We get married.

[She turns to Ludlow.]

CARLA *(CONT'D)*: So you see, it would be kind of messy if I was already married when he gets here.

LUDLOW: You know something, Carla? I sort of have a dream girl myself.

CARLA: What's she like?

LUDLOW: She's a spunky, hearty, little curly-haired spitfire, who doesn't know what's good for her.

CARLA: I hope you find her some day.

LUDLOW: Me too. And I want you to know I intend to take care of this child financially.

CARLA: You bet your buns you will, Benny Baby.

[He exits. Carla stands there considering her fate.]

APPENDIX B
SUGGESTED PLAYS AND ANTHOLOGIES

PLAYS

The following American plays are good sources of scenes with the qualities most useful for the exercises in this book. Most of these plays are available in inexpensive paperback "acting editions" from the publishers indicated.

After the Fall by Arthur Miller (Dramatists Play Service)

Ah, Wilderness! by Eugene O'Neill (Samuel French)

All My Sons by Arthur Miller (Dramatists Play Service)

The Amen Corner by James Baldwin (Samuel French)

American Buffalo by David Mamet (Samuel French)

The Andersonville Trial by Saul Levitt (Dramatists Play Service)

And Miss Reardon Drinks a Little by Paul Zindel (Dramatists Play Service)

Angels in America by Tony Kushner (Theatre Communications Group)

Anna Christie by Eugene O'Neill (Vintage Books)

Bedrooms: Five Comedies by Renee Taylor and Joseph Bologna (Samuel French)

Bent by Martin Sherman (Samuel French)

Birdbath by Leonard Melfi (Samuel French)

Born Yesterday by Garson Kanin (Dramatists Play Service)

Cat on a Hot Tin Roof by Tennessee Williams (Dramatists Play Service)

Chapter Two by Neil Simon (Samuel French)

The Chase by Horton Foote (Dramatists Play Service)

The Children's Hour by Lillian Hellman (Dramatists Play Service)

The Colored Museum by George C. Wolfe (Broadway Play Publishing)

Come Back, Little Sheba by William Inge (Samuel French)

Come Back to the 5 & Dime, Jimmy Dean, Jimmy Dean by Ed Graczyk (Samuel French)

A Coupla White Chicks Sitting Around Talking by John Ford Noonan (Samuel French)

Crimes of the Heart by Beth Henley (Dramatists Play Service)

Crossing Delancey by Susan Sandler (Samuel French)

The Crucible by Arthur Miller (Dramatists Play Service)

The Dark at the Top of the Stairs by William Inge (Dramatists Play Service)

A Day in the Death of Joe Egg by Peter Nichols (Samuel French)

Death of a Salesman by Arthur Miller (Dramatists Play Service)

The Death of Bessie Smith by Edward Albee (Plume)

A Delicate Balance by Edward Albee (Samuel French)

Division Street by Steve Tesich (Samuel French)

Duet for One by Tom Kempinski (Samuel French)

The Eccentricities of a Nightingale by Tennessee Williams (Dramatists Play Service)

Effect of Gamma Rays on Man-in-the-Moon Marigolds by Paul Zindel (Bantam)

Enter Laughing by Joseph Stein (Samuel French)

Extremities by William Mastrosimone (Samuel French)

Fences by August Wilson (Samuel French)

Fool for Love by Sam Shepard (Dramatists Play Service)

Frankie and Johnny in the Clair de Lune by Terrence McNally (Dramatists Play Service)

The Gingerbread Lady by Neil Simon (Samuel French)

The Glass Menagerie by Tennessee Williams (Dramatists Play Service)

Glengarry Glen Ross by David Mamet (Samuel French)

Golden Boy by Clifford Odets (Dramatists Play Service)

A Hatful of Rain by Michael Vincente Gazzo (Samuel French)

The Heidi Chronicles by Wendy Wasserstein (Dramatists Play Service)

The House of Blue Leaves by John Guare (Samuel French)

The Immigrant by Mark Harelik (Broadway Play Publishing)

I Never Sang for My Father by Robert Anderson (Dramatists Play Service)

I Ought to Be in Pictures by Neil Simon (Samuel French)

It Had to Be You by Renee Taylor and Joseph Bologna (Samuel French)

Last of the Red Hot Lovers by Neil Simon (Samuel French)

Last Summer at Bluefish Cove by Jane Chambers (JH Press)

Laundry and Bourbon by James McLure (Dramatists Play Service)

A Lie of the Mind by Sam Shepard (Dramatists Play Service)

The Little Foxes by Lillian Hellman (Dramatists Play Service)

Long Day's Journey into Night by Eugene O'Neill (Yale University Press)

Look Homeward, Angel by Ketti Frings (Samuel French)

Lost in Yonkers by Neil Simon (Samuel French)

Lovers and Other Strangers by Renee Taylor and Joseph Bologna (Samuel French)

Luv by Murray Schisgal (Dramatists Play Service)

The Matchmaker by Thornton Wilder (Samuel French)

The Middle Ages by A. R. Gurney, Jr. (Dramatists Play Service)

Moonchildren by Michael Weller (Samuel French)

A Moon for the Misbegotten by Eugene O'Neill (Samuel French)

Murder at the Howard Johnson's by Ron Clark and Sam Bobrick (Samuel French)

The Nerd by Larry Shue (Dramatists Play Service)

'Night, Mother by Marsha Norman (Dramatists Play Service)

The Night of the Iguana by Tennessee Williams (Dramatists Play Service)

No Place to Be Somebody by Charles Gordone (Samuel French)

The Odd Couple (Female Version) by Neil Simon (Samuel French)

The Odd Couple (Male Version) by Neil Simon (Samuel French)

Of Mice and Men by John Steinbeck (Dramatists Play Service)

Oh Dad, Poor Dad, Mamma's Hung You in the Closet and I'm Feelin' So Sad by Arthur Kopit (Samuel French)

The Only Game in Town by Frank D. Gilroy (Samuel French)

On the Open Road by Steve Tesich (Samuel French)

The Philadelphia Story by Philip Barry (Samuel French)

Picnic by William Inge (Dramatists Play Service)

The Prisoner of Second Avenue by Neil Simon (Samuel French)

The Rainmaker by N. Richard Nash (Samuel French)

A Raisin in the Sun by Lorraine Hansberry (Samuel French)

The Red Coat by John Patrick Shanley (Dramatists Play Service)

Scenes from American Life by A. R. Gurney, Jr. (Samuel French)

The Sea Horse by Edward J. Moore (Samuel French)

Sexual Perversity in Chicago by David Mamet (Samuel French)

The Shadow Box by Michael Cristofer (Samuel French)

The Sign in Sidney Brustein's Window by Lorraine Hansberry (Samuel French)

Six Degrees of Separation by John Guare (Dramatists Play Service)

Speed-the-Plow by David Mamet (Samuel French)

Splendor in the Grass by William Inge (Dramatists Play Service)

Spoils of War by Michael Weller (Samuel French)

Steel Magnolias by Robert Harling (Dramatists Play Service)

Strange Snow by Stephen Metcalfe (Samuel French)

A Streetcar Named Desire by Tennessee Williams (Dramatists Play Service)

The Subject Was Roses by Frank D. Gilroy (Samuel French)

Summer and Smoke by Tennessee Williams (Dramatists Play Service)

Sweet Bird of Youth by Tennessee Williams (Dramatists Play Service)

The Tenth Man by Paddy Chayefsky (Samuel French)

That Championship Season by Jason Miller (Samuel French)

The Time of Your Life by William Saroyan (Samuel French)

To Gillian on Her Thirty-Seventh Birthday by Michael Brady (Broadway Play Publishing)

A Touch of the Poet by Eugene O'Neill (Random House)

Toys in the Attic by Lillian Hellman (Dramatists Play Service)

Tribute by Bernard Slade (Samuel French)

True West by Sam Shepard (Samuel French)

Twice Around the Park by Murray Schisgal (Samuel French)

A View from the Bridge by Arthur Miller (Dramatists Play Service)

Vikings by Stephen Metcalfe (Samuel French)

Waiting for Lefty by Clifford Odets (Grove Press)

What I Did Last Summer by A. R. Gurney, Jr. (Dramatists Play Service)

When You Comin' Back, Red Ryder? by Mark Medoff (Dramatists Play Service)

Who's Afraid of Virginia Woolf? by Edward Albee (Dramatists Play Service)

The Women by Clare Boothe Luce (Dramatists Play Service)

Yellowman by Dael Orlandersmith (Vintage)

The Zoo Story by Edward Albee (Dramatists Play Service)

Zoot Suit and Other Plays by Luis Valdez (Arte Publico Press)

PLAY AND SCENE ANTHOLOGIES

A number of anthologies of scenes are available for student actors; they can be found in specialty book stores or online. Most of these books index scenes in a variety of ways (male-male, female-male, female-female, and by genre and ethnicity). They can be useful for picking a scene, but remember that for our purposes you must also read the entire play from which the scene comes.

One-Act Plays for Acting Students: An Anthology of Short One-Act Plays for One, Two, or Three Actors, ed. Norman Bert (Meriwether)

24 Favorite One-Act Plays, ed. Bennett Cerf, Van H. Cartmell (Main Street Books)

99 Film Scenes for Actors, ed. Angela Nicholas (Avon)

The Actor's Book of Scenes from New Plays, ed. Eric Lane (Penguin USA)

The Actor's Scenebook, ed. Michael Schulman (Bantam Books)

The Best American Short Plays 1997–1998, ed. Glenn Young (Applause Theatre Books)

The Best American Short Plays 1999–2000, ed. Glenn Young (Applause Theatre Books)

The Best American Short Plays 2000–2001, ed. Mark Glubke (Applause Theatre Books)

Duo! Best Scenes for the 90's (Applause Acting Series), ed. John Horvath, Byrna Wortman, Lavonne Mueller, Jack Temchin (Applause Theatre Books)

Duo! Best Scenes of the 90's, ed. John Horvath (Applause Theatre Books)

Famous American Plays of the 70's (The Laurel Drama Series), ed. Ted Hoffman (Laurel)

Five Comic One-Act Plays by Anton Chekhov (Dover Thrift Editions)

Great Scenes and Monologues for Actors, ed. Eva Mekler, Michael Schulman (St. Martin's Press)

Great Scenes and Monologues for Actors, ed. Michael Schulman (St. Martin's Press)

Plays for Young Audiences: An Anthology of Selected Plays for Young Audiences, ed. Max Bush, Roger Ellis (Meriwether)

Plays from the Contemporary American Theatre, ed. Brooks McNamara (Signet)

The Scenebook for Actors, ed. Norman A. Bert (Meriwether)

Scenes and Monologs from the Best New Plays, ed. Roger Ellis (Meriwether)

The Ultimate Scene and Monologue Source Book, by Ed Hooks (Backstage Books)

Wordplays 5: An Anthology of New American Drama: Plays by James Strahs, James Lapine–Stephen Sondheim, Des McAnuff, John Jesurun, Kathy Acker (PAJ)

Wordplays: An Anthology of New American Drama by Maria Fornes, Ronald Tavel, Jean-Claude Van Itallie, William Hauptman (Farrar, Straus, and Giroux)

ANTHOLOGIES FOR STUDENTS OF COLOR

Asian American Drama: 9 Plays from the Multiethnic Landscape, ed. Brian Nelson (Applause Theatre Books)

Beyond the Pale: Dramatic Writing from First Nations Writers & Writers of Color, ed. Yvette Nolan (Consortium Books)

Black Comedy: Nine Plays, ed. Pamela Faith Jackson, Karimah (Applause Theatre Books)

Black Drama in America: An Anthology, ed. Darwin T. Turner (Howard University Press)

Black Theatre USA Revised and Expanded Edition, Vol. 1: Plays by African Americans from 1847 to Today, ed. James V. Hatch, Ted Shine (Free Press)

Black Thunder: An Anthology of Contemporary African American Drama, ed. William B. Branch (Signet)

Colored Contradictions: An Anthology of Contemporary African-American Plays, ed. Robert Alexander, Harry Justin Elam (Plume Books)

Contemporary Plays by Women of Color, ed. Kathy A. Perkins (Routledge)

Drama for a New South Africa: Seven Plays, ed. David Graver (Indiana University Press)

The Fire This Time: African American Plays for the 21st Century, ed. Robert Alexander, Harry Justin Elam (Theatre Communications Group)

Great Scenes from Minority Playwrights: Seventy-Four Scenes of Cultural Diversity, ed. Marsh Cassady (Meriwether)

Latin American Theatre in Translation: An Anthology of Works from Mexico, the Caribbean and the Southern Cone, ed. Charles Philip Thomas, Marco Antonio de la Parra (Xlibris)

Moon Marked and Touched by Sun: Plays by African-American Women, ed. Sydne Mahone (Theatre Communications Group)

Multicultural Theatre II: Contemporary Hispanic, Asian and African-American Plays, ed. Roger Ellis (Meriwether)

The National Black Drama Anthology: Eleven Plays from America's Leading African-American Theaters, ed. Woodie King, Jr. (Applause Theatre Books)

Playwrights of Color, ed. Meg Swanson, Robin Murray (Intercultural Press)

Political Stages: A Dramatic Anthology, ed. Emily Mann, David Roessel (Applause Theatre Books)

Seven Black Plays: The Theodore Ward Prize for African American Playwriting, ed. Chuck Smith (Northwestern)

Seventh Generation: An Anthology of Native American Plays, ed. Mimi D'Aponte (Theatre Communications Group)

Unbroken Thread: An Anthology of Plays by Asian American Women, ed. Roberta Uno (University of Massachusetts Press)

Voices of Color: 50 Scenes and Monologues by African American Playwrights (Applause Acting Series), ed. Woodie King, Jr. (Applause Theatre Books)

War Plays by Women: An International Anthology, ed. Claire M. Tylee, Elaine Turner, Agnes Cardinal (Routledge)

GLOSSARY OF THEATER AND FILM TERMINOLOGY

Action Used in two ways. In a play or film script, the dramatic action is what happens in the story, scene, or beat in the most fundamental sense. For an actor, the action is what his or her character does to try to fulfill a need by attaining some objective. Stanislavski spoke of both spiritual (inner) and physical (outer) action. Note that speaking is one of the most common forms of action; that is, saying is also doing. To be "in action" is to be totally involved in the task at hand and is the most desirable condition for an actor. Action is the most fundamental concept behind most systems of acting. (See also *Automatic action, Choice, Indirect action, Inner action, Justify, Motivation, Objective, Reacting, Score, Stimulus, Strategic choice, Suppression,* and *Verb.*)

Ad lib To insert one's own words into a script, usually on the spur of the moment.

Agent Someone who represents and markets actors. An agent normally gets a 10 percent commission on everything an actor earns. In film and television, actors are usually auditioned only when their names are submitted by a licensed agent, so getting an agent is often the first step in initiating a professional film or television career.

The American Federation of Television and Radio Artists (AFTRA) The union that covers radio acting and some television shows that are not filmed.

Arc The movement from the low point to the high point of an action; also, the change in a character from the beginning of a play to the end.

Attitude The way a character feels about something that has happened.

Automatic action Stanislavski's term for what we call a habit or reflex; something a character does without thinking.

Beat A unit of action with its own specific conflict and crisis. In each beat a character has a single objective. Beats are formed of interactions and flow to create the underlying structure of a scene. The term may have been created by someone with a Russian accent saying "bit" of action, although it makes sense as a unit of rhythm (as in "downbeat") because the flow of the beats is the primary rhythm of a scene.

Beat change The point at which a character changes a strategy or objective, moving the scene in a new direction. A beat change results from either an automatic action or a deliberate choice made by the character.

Believability Consistency with the created reality and style of the world of the story and the personality of the character, whether like everyday life or not.

Bio (See *Résumé.*)

Blocking Establishing the positions and movements of the actors on the stage or in relation to the camera. Good blocking should express the underlying action of the scene. (See also *Mark.*)

Breakdown (See *Scenario.*)

Breath cadence (See *Cadences.*)

Cadences The levels of rhythm built into the dialogue; the flow of accented and unaccented syllables, breath phrases, and the length of speeches that form the dialogue.

Call The time an actor is to report for work. Missing a call is a serious offense. In the theater, calls are posted on the call board; in film and television, they are announced for the following day on a call sheet distributed near the end of each day's shooting.

Callback There are usually preliminary auditions in the audition process, from which a small number of actors are called back for a final audition.

Casting director Preliminary auditions, especially in film and television, are usually conducted by a casting director who then selects the actors for callbacks with the director or producer. Casting directors are extremely important to actors starting out; they can be more important to the establishment of a career than are agents.

Centeredness Although it has a literal, physical dimension, being centered implies a unified sense of self that allows actions to involve the whole body and be well focused.

Cheating out Standing so that one's face is turned slightly toward the audience or camera.

Cheating out is more important on stage than in film.

Choice When pursuing a need, a character may consider several alternative courses of action and then make a strategic choice that appears to hold out the best chance of success. Examining a character's significant choices can provide a wealth of information about the character.

Climax The "main event," which is the resolution of the underlying conflict of a story and therefore the end of the suspense. Scenes normally do not have climaxes, because the suspense of the story must carry into the next scene.

Conflict The opposition between two forces that underlies a dramatic situation and forces a movement toward resolution. Conflict can be seen on many levels—within a beat, a scene, or the entire play; between characters; or within a character.

Connotation The implications or references of a word at the time the play was written; may be different from the literal dictionary meaning, which is denotation.

Continuity In film and television, making sure that every detail of a shot matches the shots that precede or follow it. An actor has to be aware, for instance, of whether his or her right hand was over the left, how much liquid was in the glass, and so on. Continuity is the responsibility of the script supervisor, an unsung hero who remembers details like these even days later.

Costume parade The first showing of the costumes on the set and under lights for approval by the director.

Coverage In film, a scene is often shot from a wide perspective called the master; the camera is then repositioned for tighter shots called coverage, which the editor will later insert into the master. Consequently, the actor's performance in coverage must match that of the master. The close-ups, which are the most demanding on the actors, are shot hours after the master, and actors must be careful to save something for them.

Craft The body of skills and techniques applied by an effective actor; in German, literally means "power."

Creative state The condition of relaxed playfulness that some psychologists say allows for maximum creativity, when a person's inner parent allows the inner child to come out and play.

Crisis The event in a story after which the outcome becomes, in hindsight, inevitable. Before this point, the energy of the story rises in suspense; during the crisis, the outcome hangs in the balance; and after the crisis, the energy flows toward resolution. Although a crisis (or turning point) leads to a climax, it is not always the same thing as the climax and is often not the emotional high point of a story. A scene has a crisis in which the main issue of that scene is decided. A beat also has a crisis just before the beat change.

Cross An actor's movement from point A to point B. Such movements need to be justified by some inner need. There are different kinds of crosses, such as the banana, which is a slight curve so that the actor ends up cheated out.

Cue Anything that causes something else to happen. For an actor it refers to the line or event just before his or her character speaks or moves. It can also refer to a change in lighting or sound.

Cueing The way in which one line follows another. In real life we often overlap one another in speech and begin responding slightly before the other person has finished speaking. In film, overlapping is sometimes avoided because it limits the editor's ability to cut from take to take. Cueing also means helping actors learn or remember lines by prompting them.

Cue-to-cue A form of technical rehearsal in which the actors are asked to jump from light cue to light cue.

Deliberation The phase of inner action when various possible choices are considered in reaction to a stimulus.

Demonstration Bertolt Brecht's idea that the actor does not become the character completely, but rather demonstrates the character's behavior for the audience while still expressing some attitude about it. Although this may sound like indicating, the good Brechtian actor's passionate commitment to the ethical point being made gives the performance its own special kind of reality, while ordinary indicating feels merely empty and unreal.

Denotation The literal dictionary meaning of a word at the time the play was written or at the time in which the action is set.

Denouement French for "unraveling"; that final portion of a story in which the loose ends are wrapped up.

Deputy In an Equity company, a member of the cast elected to serve as the representative of the actors to the management. (See also *Equity*.)

Dialogue cadence (See *Cadences*.)

Downstage At one time, stages were sloped to enhance the illusion of perspective, so actors were literally moving "down" stage when heading toward the audience, and they were literally moving "up" stage when backing away from the audience. Even though our stages today are rarely sloped (or "raked"), we still use this terminology.

Dramatic When the outcome of an event is important and cannot be foretold, we say it is dramatic. (See also *Suspense*.)

Dramatic function The job a character was created to do within a story. It can be related to plot, meaning, an understanding of the main character, or any combination of these.

Dress rehearsal The final rehearsals that are conducted under performance conditions.

Dual consciousness An actor's ability to be immersed in a character and the character's world, while still reserving a level of awareness for artistic judgment. Different types of material make different demands on actors; film requires the virtual elimination of the actor's awareness in favor of the character's.

Economy Doing enough to fulfill the dramatic function and believability of a character but avoiding extraneous details or effort.

Emotion memory (or recall) An actor's application of a memory from his or her real or imaginary past to enrich his or her response to the situation in the scene. While this device may be useful in rehearsal, it should never be used in performance for fear of taking the actor out of the here and now.

Empathy An actor's ability to put him- or herself in the place of another person, both for purposes of observation and for applying the Magic If to a role. It is possible to empathize with someone without sympathizing with that person.

Equity The Actors Equity Association (AEA), the main theatrical union for actors. *The Equity Rule Book* establishes the conditions under which actors may work in the theater. Grievances are reported to the elected Equity deputy.

Exposition Information about what has already happened that helps an audience understand what is going on in a story or scene. The difficulty in writing or playing exposition lies in not interrupting the action by falling into an informational tone. One old piece of advice is to make exposition ammunition; that is, a character

must have a reason for providing expository information, and it must be justified by inner need.

Extra A nonspeaking actor who rounds out the reality of a scene. Professional extras in film are skilled workers who can repeat precise movements and blocking and know how to be believable without being distracting.

Eye line In film, the direction in which an actor is looking must match the spatial relationship established by the camera in the scene. Usually the other actor stands in a spot that prompts the correct eye line. When one character's eye line is close to the lens, the other actor may be pressed up against the camera. The director of photography (DP) or the camera operator guides the actors in providing the correct eye line.

Focus Whatever an actor is concentrating on at any given moment, usually the character's objective.

Functional traits Those qualities that a character was given (or that an actor provides) to allow the character to believably fulfill his or her dramatic function in the story.

Givens More completely, the given circumstances; the world and situation within which a character lives, especially as the conditions affect his or her action. The circumstances include who, when, and where.

Going up Forgetting lines. Although a terrible experience, forgetting lines can sometimes provide wonderfully rich moments if the actor keeps the action going, perhaps even resorting to paraphrase. Lines are learned more tenuously in film than on stage to guarantee the kind of freshness and authenticity the camera demands.

Head shot The glossy 8 × 10 photograph an actor hands out along with his or her résumé. The photograph should be attractive but not limiting in the way it portrays him or her—its function is merely to help someone remember the actor.

Immediacy The quality of an action or performance that makes it seem to be happening right now, before our eyes, as if for the first time.

Improvisation Performing without a script. Although most comedic improvs are based on a scenario in which the actors have some idea of the basic beats of the scene and the climax, an open-ended improv may be based on only a situation or a relationship. In traditional theater, some directors use improvisation as a rehearsal device in which the actors explore their characters in situations beyond those contained in the script.

Many good actors are terrible at improvisation, and many good improvisers are better at stand-up comedy than at characterizational acting.

In (or **out**)   On stage, a turn toward center (or away from center).

In action   (See *Action.*)

Indicating   Showing instead of doing; that is, standing outside the reality of a character and playing the emotion or some quality of the character instead of being immersed in the experience of the action.

Indirect action   When some obstacle, internal or external, impedes direct action, a character may choose an indirect strategy, saying or doing one thing while really intending another. When there is indirect action, there is also subtext. (See also *Subtext.*)

Inner action   The inner process of reaction, attitude, need, and choice that results in outer or observable action. A believable performance integrates inner and outer action into one flow of stimulus and response. This integration is called justifying the external action by connecting it to an internal process.

Inner monologue   The stream of consciousness of the character. As a training or rehearsal device, actors sometimes verbalize or at least think through their characters' inner monologues to be sure they have provided full inner justification for their external actions.

Intention   (See *Objective.*)

Interaction   One instance of give and take between characters, sometimes also called a moment. The validity of each interaction can be judged by asking two questions: First, has one character truly affected the other? Second, does this link in the chain of action and reaction move the scene in the proper direction?

Justify   To connect outer (visible or audible) actions to inner needs and processes. A script provides the basis for outer actions; however much the script may hint at the inner actions that produce the outer actions, it is ultimately the task of the actors to justify the actions. In justifying, the actors put their personal stamp on the performance.

The League of Resident Theatres (LORT)   An organization that has negotiated a specific contract with Actors Equity governing the operation of regional theaters that maintain a resident company. Being a member of a resident company, including performing in the various

summer festivals, is the best growth experience an actor can have and is the traditional stepping-stone from training to a professional career.

Magic If   Stanislavski's technique in which actors put themselves in the given circumstances of their characters as if they lived in that world, then experience their characters' needs as if they were their own, and finally choose and pursue their characters' actions as if they were their own. This process results in metamorphosis or transformation, whereby the actor becomes the character, though without losing the dual consciousness that provides artistic control. (See also *Transformation.*)

Mark   In film and television, a piece of colored tape that shows an actor where to stand at a specific moment in a scene. The actor must hit each mark without looking down.

Master   (See *Coverage.*)

Matching   In film, the need to match details and emotional tone from shot to shot. (See also *Coverage.*)

Metamorphosis   (See *Transformation.*)

Moment   A brief period of time when something of special value is happening. We speak of "making the moment." It can also refer to an interaction between characters; several interactions make up a beat.

Motivation   The inner need that drives a character's action; it usually comes from something that has just happened in a scene, although the need may be long-standing. It is important that the energy coming from a past motivation drives the character toward some objective in the immediate future because an actor can't play motivation. Motivation must lead to aspiration.

Need   Something a character lacks or wants that drives him or her to pursue an action to satisfy that lack or desire.

Objective   The goal a character pursues through action to satisfy a need. An objective is best identified using a transitive verb phrase, such as "to persuade him to give me a territory in town." In practice, the most useful form of an objective is a change in the other character, such as "to get him to look at me with compassion"; this draws the actor's energy outward and into the immediate future, bringing him or her into strong interaction with the other character. The terms *intention* and *task* are sometimes used to mean *objective.*

Off book Performed without the script; that is, with lines memorized. Immediately after going off book, it is expected that an actor will need prompting; he or she should call for lines without apology so that there is no loss of concentration or sense of action.

Pace The momentum or flow of a scene. Pace is different from tempo, which refers to the speed of the action. Regardless of tempo, a scene has good pace when the connections of cause and effect, action and reaction are strong and real so that the action flows with integrity and purpose. Paradoxically, sometimes slowing the tempo of a scene improves the pace because the actors are forced to experience the connections of action and reaction more fully.

Paraphrase To use one's own words in place of the words of the script, although with an effort to mean the same thing. Paraphrasing can sometimes help actors to examine the meaning of their lines and to "own" or personalize them. It can also help carry actors over moments in which they "go up" on their lines. In film and television, a modest amount of paraphrasing is sometimes tolerated as a way of producing a more personal performance.

Personalization The indispensable process of making a character's needs, choices, habits, and actions one's own. (See also *Magic If*.)

Playable Referring to an objective or action that is useful in performance and contributes to the movement of the scene. The most playable objectives are SIP: singular, immediate, and personally important.

Play through Let the action flow with good pace by keeping awareness moving toward a future objective and avoiding falling into internal feelings or the past. An actor's energy is most useful to a scene when it is oriented outward and toward the future.

Plot The sequence of events as the story unfolds. An actor needs to be aware of how each of his or her actions moves the plot forward, especially when a scene contains a plot point that must be solidly established.

Projection In the theater, speaking loudly enough and with enough clarity to be heard and understood throughout the auditorium. Good projection is usually more a matter of clarity than of sheer volume. In film, however, any sense of projection reads as unreal. When Michael Redgrave, already an accomplished stage actor, did his first take for a camera, he asked the director how it was. The director, who was standing behind the camera, said, "It was fine, Michael, except I could hear you."

Prompt book The copy of the script kept by the stage manager; it contains the blocking, the lighting and sound cues, and all the rest of the physical aspects of a production. It is possible to re-create a production from the prompt book, as is sometimes done in the case of great European productions. Some of Shakespeare's plays were printed from his prompt books. In film, the script supervisor records every shot in a book, permitting the editor to access particular takes in a scene.

Prompting Giving actors lines when they ask for them. Actors usually call out, "Line." Lines are given by the stage manager in a theater and by the script supervisor in film.

Prop Anything a character handles. It is wise to begin working with rehearsal substitutes as soon as actors are off book.

Public solitude Stanislavski's concept of how actors, by focusing on their objectives, can "forget" that they are in public and thereby avoid self-consciousness and stage fright. The concept does not imply that actors neglect the discipline of producing a publicly effective performance.

Raising the stakes Heightening the drama of an action or scene by making it more significant or urgent.

Reacting Responding to an immediate stimulus in a scene; allowing that stimulus to make the actor do whatever his or her character would do in response. This requires real hearing and seeing and the courage to accept the stimulus as the other actor actually provides it, rather than playing what was previously imagined. Because everything a character does is in reaction to something, we say that acting is reacting. The ideal is to be more moved than moving.

Read-through A rehearsal in which an entire scene or script is read aloud.

Recognition In Aristotle's sense, the realization of something by a character, usually something of great consequence.

Recognition Traits Qualities given a character to "round them out" as a real human being.

Reel A videotape containing a compilation of an actor's appearances on film. A reel may contain work in student films or classroom exercises. Although a reel may be useful in the early stages of a career, it is rarely worth the effort expended in making it.

Relationship All characters exist in relationship to other characters, and we come to understand characters mostly by observing the way others relate to them. For this reason, we say that actors create each other's characters more than they create their own. It is important to develop a character in specific relationship to the performances of the other actors in a scene.

Relaxation The key to almost everything in acting. For an actor, relaxation is not a reduction of energy but rather a freeing of energy and a readiness to react. The term *restful alertness* is the best description.

Repertory A company of actors that performs a body of plays. When a number of plays are performed on alternating days, it is called rotating, or true, repertory. The regional repertory movement in this country is an important source of entry-level jobs for young actors.

Résumé A listing of an actor's experience, showing the roles he or she has performed, including where and under whose direction, as well as training and special skills.

Roback Voco-Sensory Theory The theory that our language was formed partly by the meaning given to certain sounds by the physical act of pronouncing them.

Running lines Two or more actors going over their lines together; the best way to memorize lines.

Scale The "size" of a performance, determined by the demands of the performance environment, from tiny (for film) to huge (for a large auditorium). Whatever the scale, it must be justified by adjustments within the inner phase of the action.

Scenario A listing of the beats of a scene; also called a breakdown. A scenario gives the actors a sense of the underlying structure of the scene; it serves as a sort of map as they move through the journey of the scene.

Scene A section of a play that has its own main conflict and crisis. A scene usually contains one of the major events of the story and makes a major change in the plot or central relationship. In a film or television script, scenes are also determined by changes in location or lighting requirements, and each scene is given a "slug line," as in "INTERIOR LIVING ROOM—NIGHT." In some older plays, scenes are marked by the entrance of major characters; these are called "French scenes."

Score Stanislavski spoke of the score of a role as the sequence of objectives. An actor comes

to understand the logic of this sequence, and eventually this flow of action carries him or her through the role, serving as a kind of total choreography for mind and body. (See also *Spine.*)

The Screen Actors Guild (SAG) The main union for film and for television shot on film; a powerful union with over 100,000 members, 94 percent of whom are unemployed at any given moment. An aspiring actor can join the union by being hired for a union job, though this is a catch-22. Some agents represent young actors informally even before they are members of the union, thereby giving them a chance to audition for union jobs.

Sense memory (or **recall)** A memory from an actor's real or imagined past of sensations similar to those required by a scene, which can enrich the actor's response to the scene. Stanislavski believed that every cell in the body is capable of such memory and urged actors to develop their storehouse of such memories.

Set up To prepare for the punch line of a joke, the entrance of a character, or some other important event. In television sitcoms, setting up a joke is called "laying pipe." In film, a set-up is one camera position.

Shot In film or television, one piece of film from one camera position, beginning when the director calls "Action" and ending when he or she calls "Cut."

Sides Sides were small versions of a play that contained only the speeches of individual characters; these are rarely used now. In film, sides are miniature copies of the scenes to be shot on a given day and are distributed each morning by the second assistant director.

Spine Stanislavski spoke of each beat and scene in a role fitting together like the vertebrae in a spine. When an actor experiences this connectedness, the role begins to flow as if under its own power. Also called the through-line of the role; similar to the score of the role, in which the through-line is understood as a sequence of objectives.

Spiritual action Stanislavski's term for the inner phase of action, which produces physical or external action.

Spontaneity Each moment of a performance should feel as if it were happening for the first time and yet be controllable and consistent from performance to performance. Stanislavski believed that this could be achieved by rehearsing an act so fully that it becomes "automatic and therefore free"; that is, if an actor doesn't need to think about it, he or she is free to experience it afresh each time it's done.

Stage directions The indications in a script about a character's gestures, tone of voice, and so on, such as "(*He moves away angrily*)." Some teachers and directors tell actors to ignore stage directions because in some so-called acting versions of a play, the stage directions may have been inserted not by the writer but from the prompt book of an earlier production. However, many writers do provide stage directions, and actors should consider them for the information they contain about the behavior and emotion of their characters, even if that behavior eventually takes a different form in a particular production.

Stage fright Everyone gets it. The only antidote is to be fully focused on the task at hand and passionately committed to it.

Stage right (or **left)** Directions on a stage are given from the actor's point of view as he or she faces the audience; that is, stage right is audience left. In film, the director says either, "Move to your right," or "Move to camera left."

Stichomythia Short, rapid alternation of speeches within the dialogue; used as a special device in classical Greek drama.

Stimulus What a character is reacting to at any given moment. The most useful stimuli are in the immediate present, however much they may trigger needs or feelings from the character's past.

Strategic choice A character's sense of how best to pursue an objective within the given circumstances. The strategic choices a character makes express the way he or she sees the world and the other characters.

Substitution A special kind of emotion recall in which someone from an actor's real or imaginary past is substituted (in the actor's mind) for another character in a scene, to enrich the actor's response to that character. This is a dangerous device because it may take the actor out of the here and now, but with caution it may be useful.

Subtext When pursuing an objective indirectly, a character may be saying or doing one thing while really meaning another. In such cases there is a difference between the surface activity (the text) and the hidden agenda (the subtext). The character may be conscious or unconscious of the subtext; in either case it is important that the actor avoid bringing the subtext to the surface of the scene by trying to play or indicate it.

Superobjective A character's main desire in life; a life goal toward which each of his or her objectives is directed. Characters, like people in everyday life, are often unconscious of their life goals, but they pervade everything the characters do.

Suppression A choice *not* to act in response to a stimulus, but rather to "hold down" the energy the stimulus has aroused. By allowing him- or herself to feel the urge to act and then making the effort to suppress it, an actor can turn a "not doing" into a playable action. A "not doing" is useful because it helps to build suspense.

Suspense A condition in which something is about to happen but the outcome is delayed and in doubt. The more important the potential event, the more doubtful the outcome, and the longer it is delayed, the greater the suspense. It prompts the question, "What will happen?"

Syllable cadence (See *Cadences.*)

Table reading Usually the first rehearsal of a script, in which the actors sit at a table and read it aloud. During any reading, it is important that the actors try to play in relationship and experience the action of the scene, not falling into a flat, "literary" tone.

Take In film, a single shot from "Action" to "Cut." There may be many takes of a given shot until the director is satisfied. The take intended for use will be indicated by the director saying, "Print it," though several takes may be printed to give the editor a choice of performances.

Task (See *Objective.*)

Technical rehearsal In theater, the rehearsal in which the lighting, sound, and nearly completed set are first brought together under the command of the stage manager. At the technical rehearsal, the lighting and sound board operators have their first chance to rehearse their cues, and the designers are seeing the set and props in action. Great patience is required of the actors at a tech rehearsal, which is sometimes quite lengthy.

Tempo The speed at which a scene is played; not to be confused with pace. An actor must be able to justify the action at any tempo; Stanislavski would sometimes have actors play a scene at various tempos as a training exercise. Within a given tempo, there are variations that produce rhythm.

Tempo-rhythm The term used by Stanislavski to refer to the whole issue of overall tempo and the variations in tempo that produce the rhythms within a scene. He believed that the tempo-rhythms of a scene are fundamental to the correctness of the action of the scene and "all by themselves" can move an actor to the correct emotion.

Through-line (See *Spine*.)

Transaction (See *Interaction*.)

Transformation The process by which an actor begins to become the character or, more accurately, make the character his or her own. To use the language of William James, the character becomes a new "me' to be inhabited by the actor's "I." Stanislavski used the term *metamorphosis*.

Universal The quality of an action, event, or character trait that allows others to recognize and respond to it as related to their own lives.

Upstage (See *Downstage*.)

Upstaging In theater, the positioning of one actor upstage of another so that the downstage actor is forced to turn toward the upstage actor (and away from the audience) to speak. In film or theater, this term also refers to any behavior that draws attention to one actor and away from another; to be avoided.

Verb The word phrase that succinctly describes an actor's action at a given moment, such as "to persuade." Only transitive verbs are used, and all forms of the verb "to be" (such as "being angry" or "being a victim") are avoided.

Visualization An actor's ability to imagine a situation, to "see" it in the mind's eye.

Visuo-motor behavior rehearsal (VMBR) A special and effective form of rehearsal that allows an actor to visualize his or her performance under performance conditions while in a relaxed state, allowing his or her deep muscles to respond to the mental image.

INDEX

It is recommended that readers first check subject headings in the Table of Contents.